Come, South Wind

Come, South Wind

A COLLECTION
OF CONTEMPLATIVES

EDITED BY M. L. SHRADY
INTRODUCTION BY
MARTIN C. D'ARCY, S.J.

PANTHEON BOOKS

My thanks are due to the following publishers, for permission to include copyright texts: George Allen & Unwin, Ltd., for Ramón Lull, "What Sign does the Beloved Bear Upon His Banner" and Luis de León, "The Heavenly Life," quoted from E. Allison Peers, *The Mystics of Spain.* Burns, Oates & Washbourne, Ltd., for excerpts from *The Cloud of Unknowing and Other Treatises.* E. P. Dutton & Co., for excerpts from Nicholas of Cusa, *The Vision of God; Jacopone da Todi,* ed. by Evelyn Underhill, tr. by Mrs. Theodore Beck; Jan van Ruysbroeck, *The Adornment of the Spiritual Marriage,* tr. by Dom C. A. Wynschenk. Published by E. P. Dutton, Inc. Harper & Brothers, for "Mortification and Non-Attachment" from *The Spirit of St. François de Sales,* by J. P. Camus, tr. by C. F. Kelley. Copyright by Harper & Brothers. Used by permission. Excerpts from *Meister Eckhart* by Raymond B. Blakney. Copyright by Harper & Brothers. Used by permission. Methuen & Co., London, for excerpts from *The Life of Blessed Henry Suso by Himself,* tr. by J. F. Knox. The Newman Press, Westminster, Maryland, for excerpts from *On the Love of God* and *Revelations of Divine Love* by St. Bernard of Clairvaux. New Directions, for excerpts from *Seeds of Contemplation* by Thomas Merton. Copyright 1949 by Our Lady of Gethsemani Monastery, and reprinted by permission of the publisher, New Directions. Sheed & Ward, Inc., for excerpts from *Confessions of St. Augustine* in the translation of F. J. Sheed. Copyright 1943 by Sheed & Ward, Inc., New York; excerpts from *Hymns to the Church* by Gertrud von le Fort, tr. into English by Margaret Chanler, published by Sheed & Ward, Inc., New York; excerpts from *The Golden Epistle of Abbot William of Saint-Thierry,* ed. by Dom Justin McCann, published by Sheed & Ward, Inc., New York.

NIHIL OBSTAT:
Martinus S. Rushford, Ph.D.
Censor Librorum

IMPRIMATUR:
†Bryan Josephus McEntegart, D.D., LL.D.
Episcopus Bruklyniensis

BRUKLYNI
Die ii Augusti, 1957.

Editor's Note

In an anthology dealing with mystical writings, a word of caution to the lay reader with regard to some of the mystics quoted seems advisable.

Of Jan van Ruysbroeck, the Catholic Encyclopedia, vol. XIII, p. 281, has this to say: "In common with most of the German mystics Ruysbroeck starts from God and comes down to man, and thence rises again to God, showing how the two are so closely united as to become one. But here he is careful to protest: 'There where I assert that we are one in God, I must be understood in this sense that we are one in love, not in essence and Nature.' Despite this declaration, however, and other similar saving clauses scattered over his pages, some of Ruysbroeck's expressions are certainly unusual and startling. The sublimity of his subject-matter was such that it could scarcely be otherwise. His devoted friend, Gerard Groote, a trained theologian, confessed to a feeling of uneasiness over certain of his phrases and passages, and begged him to change or modify them for the sake at least of the weak. Later on, Jean Gerson and then Bossuet both professed to find traces of unconscious pantheism in his works. But as an offset to these we may mention the enthusiastic commendations of his contemporaries, Groote, Tauler, a Kempis, Scoenhoven, and in subsequent times of the Franciscan van Herp, the Carthusians Denys and Surius, the Carmelite Thomas of Jesus, the Benedictine Louis de Blois, and the Jesuit Lessius."

Of Meister Eckhart's writings, twenty-eight propositions,

drawn from his works, were condemned, after his death, by Pope John XXII.

Some of Ramón Lull's writings are considered of doubtful orthodoxy.

Needless to say, all quotations included in this volume are fully orthodox. However, with reference to the selection from Ruysbroeck entitled "How One Enters into the God-seeing Life," the comment and caution cited from the Catholic Encyclopedia must be kept firmly in mind.

Contents

9

Introduction

A reader of *Come, South Wind* might be so surprised and pleased with the beauty of the passages chosen as to stop there. But this is not just a collection of spiritual masterpieces; it is a work of art as well as of affection. It can be compared to an oratorio carefully contrived, with the main thoughts recurring like motifs in the parts and ending inevitably in the *Finale Maestoso*.

The reference in the title is to the love, from the Canticle of Canticles, of the Divine Lover, for the spouse, who is a "garden enclosed," and the theme in *Come, South Wind* tells us the nature of this love and of the revealed ways of love. The opening passages are fittingly taken from St. Anselm's *Proslogion* and St. Augustine's *Confessions*. They are very much of one spirit, the disciple and the master, and they ask the questions which God wants to answer, and so set the tone of Christian spirituality. "Teach me to seek thee and reveal thyself to me when I seek thee, for I cannot seek thee, except thou teach me, nor find thee, except thou reveal thyself." If these words come to us from the past, then there is the contemporary Thomas Merton repeating them in: "We become contemplatives when God discovers himself in us." The next movements tell us of God with us and in us, God made flesh and living in his mystical body, the Church and in the world. The response to this exodus of God is seen in the next movements, the exodus of the soul. The tessara is *Egredere, Egredere*, the need of dying to self in order

13

to penetrate into the Darkness of Beyond Being and to enter the Cloud of Unknowing. This state of unknowing does not, however, lead to self-annihilation, nor to the denial of creatures and their loveliness; for "If I come forth by way of Touch, On every creature fair In sacred awe I lay my hands, For Thou art sculptured there" (Jacopone da Todi). Action, too, and contemplation go together in the fertile union of the soul with God; for, as Tauler says of the true contemplatives: "To all men they give benefit, to God glory, and to all things comfort." The theme then draws to its end with passages on The Holy Week of Our Life and The Day without Evening, and closes with the Anaphora of the Syrian Liturgy, a eucharistic hymn of praise.

The theme covers the Christian way and truth, not like a work of theology nor as a set of spiritual exercises. It gives us a vision of what has been revealed by God through the medium of the prayers, aspirations and contemplation of the saints, the poets and the liturgy. They have been worked into a composition of great variety; the rarefied meditations of a Ruysbroeck and a Tauler are set off by the poems of a Jacopone da Todi or Mechthild of Magdeburg and "flowers" from the Franciscan annals. Translations by the editor of Père Gratry mingle with St. Bernard, Gertrude von Le Fort, and Roy Campbell's translations of St. John of the Cross. Two of the most pleasing surprises are an extract from the *Golden Epistle* of William of St. Thierry and the Blessing of the Paschal Candle from the liturgy of Holy Saturday.

I have read many selections from the writings of the great Catholic spiritual masters and mystics, but never felt before so joyfully their intimate family likeness and their personal traits—nor again the far-stretching but clearly defined wisdom they both taught and lived.

Our knowledge of the religions of the East, their ideals and methods, has made a great advance in the last fifty years, as translations and commentaries have multiplied. The late Ananda Coomaraswamy has told us that Asia "has consistently and consciously acted in an awareness that the goal is only reached when the knower and the known, subject and object, are identified in one experience," that "in India is has been a cardinal principle of devotion that to worship God one must become God" (Introduction to his *Art of Eastern Asia,* p. 13). Mr. Aldous Huxley corroborates this judgment in his introduction to his Mentor Book *The Song of God: Bhagavad-Gita.* He believes that there is a common wisdom, a highest common factor, to be found in all high religions. It consists in this, that there is a divine ground of which man and nature are manifestations, and man by denying his lower self can know this divine ground and pass into identity with it.

This view of human life and of the ideal for human persons is said to be also the teaching of Christianity, and as evidence for this the Christian mystics are quoted. But however similar at times the language may be—and it must be remembered that both Asian and Western mystics are attempting to describe what is beyond ordinary experience and its language—the Christian holds fast to humanity and human personality and to the unbridgeable difference between the living God and finite beings. On this the teaching of Christianity never wavers. The Christian Christ is not, as Aldous Huxley supposes, a manifestation, like Krishna or Gotama, of the divine reality. He is a man who suffered under Pontius Pilate, a man who is God Himself, through whom and in whom a loving relationship is set between God and human individuals. Persons grow in the intimacies of love and in such a love they are transfigured, not dissolved. If then the word "identity" be used by Christian mystics it never means that love has destroyed distinctness, and the reader will see how true this is in the pages which follow.

In the mysterious world of mysticism we can perhaps distinguish three forms. There is first natural mysticism. The mystic feels himself drawn into the dark and losing his identity in some mysterious center or ground or whole, with nature felt as a mother and often symbolized in a goddess. Modern psychology can tell us much about this, and I have tried to explain it in *The Mind and Heart of Love*. Secondly, there is solitary mysticism, which may contain some of the features of the first kind but is distinct in that it is strictly religious and its goal is identity with the highest, with what is meant at times by God. It has its own discipline and techniques, and its language is of great beauty. But for the reason that it is a solitary experience it is subjective, and in the dark the light it gives does not show the real landscape. There is no company, no voice to give bearings, no presence to bring the self to itself and another. "You can do as you will with solitude," says one of I. Compton-Burnett's characters. "It does not take you on equal terms." The solitary mystic discards knowledge and loses himself, and this is different from love which has issued from knowledge and is still soaked in it.

The third form of mysticism is the Christian, which is the agape of persons. Knowledge and affection are never completely separated, and in the love of persons there is no diminution on either side, but gain and increase. Mr. Ralph Harper in *The Sleeping Beauty* says very truly that "the only adequate cure for anonymity is the gift of presence." The Christian mystic keeps alive in the abiding presence of Christ and if he speaks of identification it is as of the Bride with the Bridegroom. "To be a person is to be essentially in search of a person. Love presupposes knowledge, but it can to some degree do without it; what it needs is the living and actual being itself. For a person there must be a person."

M. C. D'Arcy, S. J.

The whole life of the good Christian is a holy desire.

Tell the lover and he will know what I mean: tell the one who desires, the one who hungers: tell the wanderer in the desert, tell him who thirsts and yearns for the fountain of his eternal country: tell such a one and he will know what I mean. But if I speak to the cold of heart they will not understand.

And with all this, what have I said, my God and my Life and my sacred Delight? What can anyone say when he speaks of Thee? Yet woe to them that speak not of Thee at all, since those who say most are but dumb.

St. Augustine

I

Thee God I Come From

*Knowledge of ourselves teaches us whence
we come, where we are and whither we are
going. We come from God and we are in
exile; and it is because our potency of affection tends towards God that we are
aware of this state of exile.*

Jan van Ruysbroeck

*A body tends by its weight towards the
place proper to it—weight does not necessarily tend towards the lowest place but
towards its proper place. Fire tends upwards, stone downwards. By their weight
they are moved and seek their proper place.
. . . Things out of their place are in motion: they come to their place and are at
rest. My love is my weight: wherever I go
my love is what brings me there.*

St. Augustine

Exhortation of the Mind to the
Contemplation of God

Up now, slight man! flee, for a little while, thy occupations; hide thyself, for a time, from thy disturbing thoughts. Cast aside, now, thy burdensome cares, and put away thy toilsome business. Yield room for some little time to God; and rest for a little time in him. Enter the inner chamber of thy mind; shut out all thoughts save that of God, and such as can aid thee in seeking him; close thy door and seek him. Speak now, my whole heart! speak now to God, saying, I seek thy face; thy face, Lord, will I seek. And come thou now, O Lord my God, teach my heart where and how it may seek thee, where and how it may find thee.

Lord, if thou art not here, where shall I seek thee, being absent? But if thou art everywhere, why do I not see thee present? Truly thou dwellest in unapproachable light. But where is unapproachable light, or how shall I come to it? Or who shall lead me to that light and into it, that I may see thee in it? Again, by what marks, under what form, shall I seek thee? I have never seen thee, O Lord, my God; I do not know thy form. What, O most high Lord, shall this man do, an exile far from thee? What shall thy servant do, anxious in his love of thee, and cast out afar from thy face? He pants to see thee, and thy face is too far from him. He longs to come to thee, and thy dwelling-place is inaccessible. He is eager to find thee, and knows not thy place. He desires to seek thee, and does not know thy face. Lord, thou art my God, and thou art my

Lord, and never have I seen thee. It is thou that hast made me, and hast made me anew, and hast bestowed upon me all the blessings I enjoy; and not yet do I know thee. Finally, I was created to see thee, and not yet have I done that for which I was made.

O wretched lot of man, when he hath lost that for which he was made! O hard and terrible fate! Alas, what has he lost, and what has he found? What has departed, and what remains? He has lost the blessedness for which he was made, and has found the misery for which he was not made. That has departed without which nothing is happy, and that remains which, in itself, is only miserable. Man once did eat the bread of angels, for which he hungers now; he eateth now the bread of sorrows, of which he knew not then. Alas! for the mourning of all mankind, for the universal lamentation of the sons of Hades! He choked with satiety, we sigh with hunger. He abounded, we beg. He possessed in happiness, and miserably forsook his possession; we suffer want in unhappiness, and feel a miserable longing, and alas! we remain empty.

Why did he not keep for us, when he could so easily, that whose lack we should feel so heavily? Why did he shut us away from the light, and cover us over with darkness? With what purpose did he rob us of life, and inflict death upon us? Wretches that we are, whence have we been driven out; whither are we driven on? Whence hurled? Whither consigned to ruin? From a native country into exile, from the vision of God into our present blindness, from the joy of immortality into the bitterness and horror of death. Miserable exchange of how great a good, for how great an evil! Heavy loss, heavy grief, heavy all our fate!

But alas! wretched that I am, one of the sons of Eve, far removed from God! What have I undertaken? What have

I accomplished? Whither was I striving? How far have I come? To what did I aspire? Amid what thoughts am I sighing? I sought blessings, and lo! confusion. I strove toward God, and I stumbled on myself. I sought calm in privacy, and I found tribulation and grief, in my inmost thoughts. I wished to smile in the joy of my mind, and I am compelled to frown by the sorrow of my heart. Gladness was hoped for, and lo! a source of frequent sighs!

And thou too, O Lord, how long? How long, O Lord, dost thou forget us; how long dost thou turn thy face from us? When wilt thou look upon us, and hear us? When wilt thou enlighten our eyes, and show us thy face? When wilt thou restore thyself to us? Look upon us, Lord; hear us, enlighten us, reveal thyself to us. Restore thyself to us, that it may be well with us,—thyself, without whom it is so ill with us. Pity our toilings and strivings toward thee, since we can do nothing without thee. Thou dost invite us; do thou help us. I beseech thee, O Lord, that I may not lose hope in sighs, but may breathe anew in hope. Lord, my heart is made bitter by its desolation; sweeten thou it, I beseech thee, with thy consolation. Lord, in hunger I began to seek thee; I beseech thee that I may not cease to hunger for thee. In hunger I have come to thee; let me not go unfed. I have come in poverty to the Rich, in misery to the Compassionate; let me not return empty and despised. And if, before I eat, I sigh, grant, even after sighs, that which I may eat. Lord, I am bowed down and can only look downward; raise me up that I may look upward. My iniquities have gone over my head; they overwhelm me; and, like a very heavy load, they weigh me down. Free me from them; unburden me, that the pit of iniquities may not close over me.

Be it mine to look up to thy light, even from afar, even from the depths. Teach me to seek thee, and reveal thyself to me, when I seek thee, for I cannot seek thee, except thou teach me, nor find thee, except thou reveal thyself. Let me seek thee in longing, let me long for thee in seeking; let me find thee in love, and love thee in finding. Lord, I acknowledge and I thank thee that thou hast created me in this thine image, in order that I may be mindful of thee, may conceive of thee, and love thee; but that image has been so consumed and wasted away by vices, and obscured by the smoke of wrong-doing, that it cannot achieve that for which it was made, except thou renew it, and create it anew. I do not endeavor, O Lord, to penetrate thy sublimity, for in no wise do I compare my understanding with that; but I long to understand in some degree thy truth, which my heart believes and loves. For I do not seek to understand that I may believe, for I believe in order to understand. For this also I believe,—that unless I believe, I should not understand.

St. Anselm of Canterbury

How Can I Call Unto My God?

Great art Thou, O Lord, and greatly to be praised; great is Thy power, and of Thy wisdom there is no number. And man desires to praise Thee. He is but a tiny part of all that Thou hast created. He bears about him his mortality, the evidence of his sinfulness, and the evidence that Thou dost resist the proud: yet this tiny part of all that Thou hast created desires to praise Thee.

Thou dost so excite him that to praise Thee is his joy. For Thou hast made us for Thyself and our hearts are restless till they rest in Thee. Grant me, O Lord, to know which is the soul's first movement toward Thee—to implore Thy aid or to utter its praise of Thee; and whether it must know Thee before it can implore. For it would seem clear that no one can call upon Thee without knowing Thee, for if he did he might invoke another than Thee, knowing Thee not. Yet it may be that a man must implore Thee before he can know Thee? But, how shall they call on Him in Whom they have not believed? or how shall they believe without a preacher? And, they shall praise the Lord that seek Him; for those that seek shall find; and finding Him they will praise Him. Let me seek Thee, Lord, by praying Thy aid, and let me utter my prayer believing in Thee: for Thou hast been preached to us. My faith, Lord, cries to Thee, the faith that Thou hast given me, that Thou hast inbreathed in me, through the humanity of Thy Son and by the ministry of Thy Preacher.

But how can I call unto my God, my God and Lord? For in calling unto Him, I am calling Him to me: and what room is there in me for my God, the God who made heaven and earth? Is there anything in me, O God, that can contain You? All heaven and earth cannot contain You for You made them, and me in them. Yet, since nothing that is could exist without You, You must in some way be in all that is: [therefore also in me, since I am]. And if you are already in me, since otherwise I should not be, why do I cry to You to enter into me? Even if I were in Hell You would be there, for if I go down into hell, Thou art there also. Thus, O God, I should be nothing, utterly nothing, unless You were in me—or rather unless I were in You, of Whom and by Whom and in Whom are all things. So it is, Lord; so it is. Where do I call You to come to, since I am in You? Or where else are

You that You can come to me? Where shall I go, beyond
the bounds of heaven and earth, that God may come to me,
since He has said: Heaven and earth do I fill.

St. Augustine

God Speaks His Name in the
Center of Our Soul

There exists some point at which I can meet God in a
real and experimental contact with His infinite actuality:
and it is the point where my contingent being depends
upon His love. Within myself is a metaphorical apex of
existence at which I am held in being by my Creator.

God utters me like a word containing a thought of
Himself.

A word will never be able to comprehend the voice that
utters it.

But if I am true to the concept that God utters in me,
if I am true to the thought of Him I was meant to em-
body, I shall be full of His actuality and find Him everywhere in myself, and find myself nowhere. I shall be lost
in Him.

What one of you can enter into himself and find the
God Who utters him?

If, like the mystics of the Orient, you succeed in empty-
ing your mind of every thought and every desire, you may
indeed withdraw into the center of yourself and concentrate everything within you upon the imaginary point
where your life springs out of God: yet you will not find
God. No natural exercise can bring you into vital contact
with Him. Unless He utters Himself in you, speaks His

own name in the center of your soul, you will no more
know Him than a stone knows the ground upon which it
rests in its inertia.

Our discovery of God is, in a way, God's discovery of
us. We cannot go to heaven to find Him because we have
no way of knowing where heaven is or what it is. He comes
down from heaven and finds us. He looks at us from the
depths of His own infinite actuality, which is everywhere,
and His seeing us gives us a superior reality in which we
also discover Him. We only know Him in so far as we
are known by Him, and our contemplation of Him is a
participation of His contemplation of Himself.

We become contemplatives when God discovers Himself in us.

At that moment, the point of our contact with Him
opens out and we pass through the center of our own
souls, and enter eternity.

Thomas Merton

The Capacity Which Maketh Union Possible
Is Likeness

Lord, Thy glance is love. And just as Thy gaze beholdeth
me so attentively that it never turneth aside from me,
even so is it with Thy love. And since it is deathless, it
abideth ever with me, and Thy love, Lord, is naught else
but Thy very Self, who lovest me. Hence Thou art ever
with me, Lord; Thou desertest me not, Lord; on all sides
Thou guardest me, for that Thou takes most diligent care
for me. Thy Being, Lord, letteth not go of my being. I
exist in that measure in which Thou art with me, and

since Thy look is Thy Being, I am because Thou dost look at me, and if Thou didst turn Thy glance from me I should cease to be.

But I know that Thy glance is that supreme Goodness which cannot fail to communicate itself to all able to receive it. Thou, therefore, canst never let me go so long as I am able to receive Thee. Wherefore it behoveth me to make myself, in so far as I can, ever more able to receive Thee. But I know that the capacity which maketh union possible is naught else save likeness. And incapacity springeth from lack of likeness. If, therefore, I have rendered myself by all possible means like unto Thy goodness, then, according to the degree of that likeness, I shall be capable of the truth.

Lord, Thou hast given me my being, of such a nature that it can make itself continually more able to receive Thy grace and goodness. And this power, which I have of Thee, wherein I possess a living image of Thine almighty power, is freewill. By this I can either enlarge or restrict my capacity for Thy grace. The enlarging is by conformity with Thee, when I strive to be good because Thou art good, to be just because Thou art just, to be merciful because Thou art merciful; when all my endeavor is turned toward Thee because all Thy endeavor is turned toward me; when I look unto Thee alone with all my attention, nor ever turn aside the eyes of my mind, because Thou dost enfold me with Thy constant regard; when I direct my love toward Thee alone because Thou, who art Love's self, hast turned Thee toward me alone. And what, Lord, is my life, save that embrace wherein Thy delightsome sweetness doth so lovingly enfold me? I love my life supremely because Thou art my life's sweetness.

Now I behold as in a mirror, in an icon, in a riddle, life

eternal, for that is naught other than that blessed regard
wherewith Thou never ceasest most lovingly to behold
me, yea, even the secret places of my soul. With Thee, to
behold is to give life; it is unceasingly to impart sweetest
love of Thee; it is to inflame me to love of Thee by love's
imparting, and to feed me by inflaming, and by feeding
to kindle my yearnings, and by kindling to make me drink
of the dew of gladness, and by drinking to infuse in me a
fountain of life, and by infusing to make it increase and
endure. It is to cause me to share Thine immortality, to
endow me with the glory imperishable of Thy heavenly
and most high and most mighty kingdom, it is to make me
partaker of that inheritance which is only of Thy Son, to
establish me in possession of eternal bliss. There is the
source of all delights that can be desired; not only can
naught better be thought out by men and angels, but
naught better can exist in any mode of being! For it is
the absolute maximum of every desire, than which a
greater cannot be.

Nicholas of Cusa

The Goodness of the All-transcendent Godhead

For as the goodness of the all-transcendent Godhead
reaches from the sublimest and highest forms of being to the
lowest, and is still above them all, being superior to those
above and embracing those below, and so sends forth light
to all things that can receive it, and creates and vitalizes
and keeps and perfects them, and is the measure of the
universe, its eternity, its harmony, its course, its reason, and
its end: thus this mighty and ever-shining sun, which is

the visible image of divine goodness, faintly re-echoing the activity of the good, enlightens all things that can receive its light, while retaining the utter simplicity of light, and expands above and below throughout the visible world the rays of its radiance. And if there is anything that does not participate therein, this is due not to any weakness or defect in the distribution of the light, but to the unreceptiveness of those creatures who do not reach sufficient singleness to share in it. For indeed the light passes over many such substances and illuminates those which are beyond them, and there is no visible thing which it does not reach in the exceeding greatness of its own radiance.

Dionysius the Areopagite[1]

[1] *De divinis nominibus.*

I Am the Food of Grown Men

Being admonished by all this to return to myself, I entered into my own depths, with You as guide; and I was able to do it because You were my helper. I entered, and with the eye of my soul, such as it was, I saw Your unchangeable Light shining over that same eye of my soul, over my mind. It was not the light of everyday that the eye of the flesh can see, nor some greater light of the same order, such as might be if the brightness of our daily light should be seen shining with a more intense brightness and filling all things with its greatness. Your Light was not that, but other, altogether other, than all such lights. Nor was it above my mind as oil above the water it floats on, nor as the sky is above the earth; it was above because it made me, and I was below because made by it. He who knows the truth knows that Light, and he that knows the Light knows eternity. Charity knows it. O eternal truth and true love and beloved eternity! Thou art my God, I sigh to Thee by day and night. When first I knew Thee, Thou didst lift me up so that I might see that there was something to see, but that I was not yet the man to see it. And Thou didst beat back the weakness of my gaze, blazing upon me too strongly, and I was shaken with love and with dread. And I knew that I was far from Thee in the region of unlikeness, as if I heard Thy voice from on high: "I am the food of grown men: grow and you shall eat Me. And you shall not change Me into yourself as bodily food, but into Me you shall be changed." And I learned that Thou hast corrected man for iniquity and Thou didst make my soul shrivel up like a moth. And I said "Is truth then nothing at all, since it is not extended either through finite spaces or infinite?" And Thou didst cry to me from afar: "I am who am." And I heard Thee, as one hears in the heart; and there was from that moment no ground of doubt in me: I would more easily have doubted my own life than have doubted that truth is: which is clearly seen, being understood by the things that are made.

St. Augustine

II

The Incarnation

Until then they had gone astray, seeking their country; but led by Christ they could not err. That way was lighted by the vision of God.

St. Augustine

For through the mystery of the Word made flesh Thy splendour has shone before our mind's eye with a new radiance, and through him whom we recognize as God made visible we are carried away in love of things invisible.

Roman Liturgy—Preface
of Our Lord's Nativity

The Mediator

And I marvelled to find that at last I loved You and not
some phantom instead of You; yet I did not stably enjoy
my God, but was ravished to You by Your beauty, yet
soon was torn away from You again by my own weight,
and fell again with torment to lower things. Carnal habit
was that weight. Yet the memory of You remained with
me and I knew without doubt that it was You to whom
I should cleave, though I was not yet such as could cleave
to You: for the corruptible body is a load upon the soul,
and the earthly habitation presses down the mind that
muses upon many things. I was altogether certain that
Your invisible things are clearly seen from the creation of
the world, being understood by the things that are made:
so too are Your everlasting power and Your Godhead. I
was now studying the ground of my admiration for the
beauty of bodies, whether celestial or of earth, and on
what authority I might rightly judge of things mutable
and say: "This ought to be so, that not so." Enquiring
then what was the source of my judgement, when I did
so judge I had discovered the immutable and true eternity
of truth above my changing mind. Thus by stages I passed
from bodies to the soul which uses the body for its per-
ceiving, and from this to the soul's inner power, to which
the body's senses present external things, as indeed the
beasts are able; and from there I passed on to the reason-
ing power, to which is referred for judgement what is
received from the body's senses. This too realised that it

was mutable in me, and rose to its own understanding. It withdrew my thought from its habitual way, abstracting from the confused crowds of fantasms that it might find what light suffused it, when with utter certainty it cried aloud that the immutable was to be preferred to the mutable, and how it had come to know the immutable itself: for if it had not come to some knowledge of the immutable, it could not have known it as certainly preferable to the mutable. Thus in the thrust of a trembling glance my mind arrived at That Which Is. Then indeed I saw clearly Your invisible things which are understood by the things that are made; but I lacked the strength to hold my gaze fixed, and my weakness was beaten back again so that I returned to my old habits, bearing nothing with me but a memory of delight and a desire as for something of which I had caught the fragrance but which I had not yet the strength to eat.

So I set about finding a way to gain the strength that was necessary for enjoying You. And I could not find it until I embraced the Mediator between God and man, the man Christ Jesus, who is over all things, God blessed forever, who was calling unto me and saying: I am the Way, the Truth, and the Life; and who brought into union with our nature that Food which I lacked the strength to take: for the Word was made flesh that Your Wisdom, by which You created all things, might give suck to our souls' infancy. For I was not yet lowly enough to hold the lowly Jesus as my God, nor did I know what lesson His embracing of our weakness was to teach. For Your Word, the eternal Truth, towering above the highest parts of Your creation, lifts up to Himself those that were cast down. He built for Himself here below a lowly house of our clay, that by it He might bring down from themselves and

bring up to Himself those who were to be made subject,
healing the swollenness of their pride and fostering their
love: so that their self-confidence might grow no further
but rather diminish, seeing the deity at their feet,
humbled by the assumption of our coat of human nature:
to the end that weary at last they might cast themselves
down upon His humanity and rise again in its rising.

St. Augustine

The Christian Way of Ascent

However high Eros may lift man by desire, the desire
remains a finite yearning, and the closer man comes to the
dark and inaccessible region of the All or the absolute the
less hold can he have on his own infinitesimal being and
existence. But the Christian does not begin with his own
craving and rely on his own technique; he begins through
an adoption into the life of Christ, and as it were, sees in
and through this medium. Christ is not the object, but
the way and the life; His humanity does not block our
vision of God, because Christ is the Companion who first
passed through the veil. We see *with* His eyes and love.
This grace can be spoken of in terms of fellowship or
communion or membership, and it continually gives life
more abundantly to the graced person. He goes down in
humility and rises in more and more abundant new
strength, so that far from being absorbed into the divinity,
he enjoys a relationship far richer than that which can be
promised by any technique of fusion. St. Paul summed
up this unique way of ascent at the very beginning when
he wrote that, . . . "Ye are dead, and your life is hid with

Christ in God." And this is also the reason why we can find the first phase, the death-motif, in a mystic . . . like Ruysbroeck: ("We long to be a stool beneath the feet of the power of God; so shall we have an humble ear to listen to the truth and life which come from the wisdom of God and a ready hand to do His most beloved will"); and the second phase of hidden life in de Bérulle: "Our first movement must be towards Jesus, as our fulfilment, and in this seeking for Jesus, in this adherence to Jesus, in this continual and profound dependence upon Jesus, is our life, our rest, our strength and all our power of working. . . ."

M. C. D'Arcy, S.J.[1]

The Glass of His Humanity

As a magnifying glass concentrates the rays of the sun into a little burning knot of heat that can set fire to a dry leaf or a piece of paper, so the mysteries of Christ in the Gospel concentrate the rays of God's light and fire to a point that sets fire to the spirit of man. And this is why Christ was born and lived in the world and died and returned from death and ascended to His Father in heaven: *ut dum visibiliter Deum cognoscimus, per hunc in invisibilium amorem rapiamur.* Through the glass of His Humanity He concentrates the rays of His Holy Spirit upon us so that we feel the burn, and all mystical experience is infused into the soul through the Man Christ.

For God is everywhere. His truth and His love pervade all things as the light and the heat of the sun pervade our

[1] *The Mind and Heart of Love.*

atmosphere. But just as the rays of the sun do not set fire to anything by themselves, so God does not touch our souls with the fire of supernatural knowledge and experience without Christ.

But the glass of that Humanity seeks out spirits that are well prepared, dried by the light and warmth of God, and ready to take flame in the little knot of fire that is the grace of the Holy Ghost.

Thomas Merton

In Christ We Possess All Things

God, in giving us, as He hath done, His Son, Who is His only Word, has spoken to us once for all by His own and only Word, and has nothing further to reveal. . . . God has now so spoken that nothing remains unspoken; for that which He partially revealed to the prophets, He hath now wholly revealed in Him, giving unto us all, that is, His Son. And therefore he who should now inquire of God in the ancient way, seeking visions and revelations, would offend Him; because he does not fix his eye upon Christ alone, disregarding all besides. To such a one the answer of God is: "This is My beloved Son, in whom I am well pleased, hear ye Him." I have spoken all by My Word, My Son; fix thine eyes upon Him, for in Him I have spoken and revealed all, and thou wilt find in Him more than thou desirest or askest. He is My whole voice and answer, My whole vision and revelation, which I spoke, answered, made and revealed when I gave Him to be thy brother, master, companion, ransom and reward. I descended upon Him with My Spirit on Mount Tabor, and said: "This is My beloved Son, in whom I am well pleased, hear ye Him." . . . While thou hast Christ thou hast nothing to ask of Me. . . . Look well unto Him, and thou wilt find that I have given all in Christ. If thou desirest a word of consolation from My mouth, behold My Son obedient to Me and afflicted for My love, and thou wilt see how great is the answer I give thee. If thou desire to learn of God secret things, fix thine eyes upon Christ, and thou wilt find the profoundest mysteries, the wisdom and marvels of God hidden in Him: "in Whom," saith the Apostle, "are hid all the treasures of wisdom and knowledge." These treasures will be sweeter and more profitable to thee than all those things thou desirest to know. It was in these that the Apostle gloried when he said: "I judged not myself to know anything among you but Jesus Christ and Him crucified." . . . Look upon His Sacred Humanity and thou wilt find there more than can ever enter into thy thoughts, "for in Him dwelleth all the fulness of the Godhead corporally."

St. John of the Cross[1]

[1] *The Ascent of Mount Carmel.*

The Heavenly Life

Fair land of radiant light,
Fields of the blest, to winter's frost unknown
And the sun's scorching might;
Soil ever newly sown,
Bearing eternal joy unto its own:

See the Good Shepherd come!
Snow-white and purple blooms enwreathe His head,
As to their heavenly home,
To fields well-watered,
Staffless and slingless His lov'd flocks are led.

He leads His sheep on high
Till, glad at heart, their pasture-land they view,
Where roses cannot die
And flow'rs are fresh with dew,
For ever cropp'd and yet for ever new.

Within the mountain's fold,
Faithful, He bathes them in the torrent's flood,
Laves them in joy untold,
Gives them abundant food:
Shepherd and Pasture He, and all their Good.

And when at length the sun
Has reached the zenith of his mighty sphere,
The hour of rest begun,
He to His flock draws near,
And with sweet sound delights His sacred ear.

He strikes the sonorous lyre,
And lo! the soul thrills to its deathless strain!
Dissolving in its fire,
It counts pure gold but vain,
Plunging within it ever and again.

O sound! O voice divine!
Might some faint note of this descend to me,
Transport my will in Thine,
Unite it utterly
Until it blend, O heavenly Love, in Thee!

Dear Love, did I but know
The pasture where Thy noontide rest would be,
I'd break my toils below,
And never stray from Thee,
But with Thy flock remain, for ever free.

Luis de León

III

The Mystical Body of Christ

*Let us be glad and give thanks that we are
made not merely Christians, but Christ. Do
you understand, my brethren? Do you take
in the grace of God put upon us? . . . We
are made Christ. For if He be the Head, we
the members; the whole Man is, He and
we. . . . The fullness of Christ is, Head
and members. . . . Christ and the Church.*

St. Augustine

*The graces of prayer and the mystical states
have their type and source in the hieratic
life of the Church, they refract in the members the light of the Image of Christ which
exists perfectly in His Body.*

Humbert Clérissac

Ut sint consummati in unum

It is the Spirit of God that must teach us Who Christ is and form Christ in us and transform us into other Christs. For after all, transformation into Christ is not just an individual affair: there is only one Christ, not many. He is not divided. And for me to become Christ is to enter into the Life of the Whole Christ, the Mystical Body made up of the Head and the members, Christ and all who are incorporated in Him by His Spirit.

But if each individual arrived at perfection by imitating his own peculiar idea of Christ there would be no One Christ, no Mystical Body. For everyone has a different idea of Christ and many of the ideas are not only opposed but contradictory. It would never be possible to reduce them all to unity.

Christ forms Himself by grace and faith in the souls of all who love Him, and at the same time He draws them all together in Himself to make them One in Him. *Ut sint consummati in unum.*

And the Holy Ghost, Who is the life of this One Body, dwells entire in the whole Body and in every one of the members so that the whole Christ is Christ and each individual is Christ.

Therefore if you want to have in your heart the affections and dispositions that were those of Christ on earth consult not your own imagination but faith. Enter into

47

the darkness of interior renunciation, strip your soul of images and let Christ form Himself in you by His cross.

Thomas Merton

Return to the Church

I have fallen on the Law of your Faith as on a naked sword.
Its sharpness went through my understanding, straight through the light of my reason.
Never again shall I walk under the star of my eyes and on the staff of my strength.
You have torn away my shores, you have done violence to the earth under my feet.
My ships are drifting out to sea, you have cut all their moorings.
The chains of my thoughts are broken, they hang wild over the deep.
I flutter like a bird about my father's house, to find a crack that will let your strange light through.
But there is none on earth save the wound in my spirit—
I have fallen on the Law of your Faith as on a naked sword.

But strength still goes out from your thorns, and from your abysses the sound of music.
Your shadows lie on my heart like roses and your nights are like strong wine.
I will love you even when my love of you is ended.
I will desire you even when I desire you no more.
Where I myself begin, there will I cease, and where I cease, there I will forever remain.
Where my feet refuse to take me, there will I kneel down.
And where my hands fail me, there I will fold them.

I will become a breath in the autumn of pride, and snow in
the winter of doubt.

Even as in graves of snow shall all fear sleep in me.

I will become dust before the rock of your teaching and ashes
in the flame of your commandments.

I will break my arms if I may clasp you with their shadow.

And behold, the voice of your commandment speaks to me:

What I break is not broken and what I bend down to the
dust that I raise up.

I have been without grace to you because of grace, and out of
compassion I have been pitiless.

I have dazzled and blinded you till your borders are effaced.

I have overshadowed you that you may no longer find your
defences.

As an island is swallowed by the sea so have I engulfed you
that I might float you into eternity.

I have become a mock to your understanding and a violence
to your nature,

That I might bolt and bar you like a prison and drag you
before the gates of your spirit.

For where your inmost thirst would take you, the fountains
of earth have ceased to flow,

Where your last nostalgia fades blue, all the clocks of time are
stopped.

See, I carry on my wings the white shadows of otherness,

And my forehead feels the breath of another shore.

It is for this that I must be a wilderness to your reason, and
a nothingness on your lips,

But to your soul I am the start and the way home, I am the
rainbow of her peace with God above the clouds.

Gertrud von Le Fort

I It Am

And after this our Lord shewed Himself more glorified, as to my sight, than I saw Him before [in the Shewing] wherein I was learned that our soul shall never have rest till it cometh to Him, knowing that He is fulness of joy, homely and courteous, blissful and very life.

Our Lord Jesus oftentimes said: *I it am, I it am: I it am that is highest, I it am that thou lovest, I it am that thou enjoyest, I it am that thou servest, I it am that thou longest for, I it am that thou desirest, I it am that thou meanest, I it am that is all. I it am that Holy Church preacheth and teacheth thee, I it am that shewed me here to thee.* The number of the words passeth my wit and all my understanding and all my powers. And they are the highest, as to my sight: for therein is comprehended—I cannot tell,—but the joy that I saw in the Shewing of them passeth all that heart may wish for and soul may desire. Therefore the words be not declared here; but every man after the grace that God giveth him in understanding and loving, receive them in our Lord's meaning. . . .

And He willeth that we take us mightily to the Faith of Holy Church and find there our dearworthy Mother, in solace of true Understanding, with all the blessed Common. For one single person may oftentimes be broken, as it seemeth to himself, but the whole Body of Holy Church was never broken, nor never shall be, without end. And therefore a sure thing it is, a good and a gracious, to will meekly and mightily to be fastened and oned to our

Mother, Holy Church, that is, Christ Jesus. For the food of mercy that is His dearworthy blood and precious water is plenteous to make us fair and clean; the blessed wounds of our Saviour be open and enjoy to heal us; the sweet, gracious hands of our Mother be ready and diligently about us. For He in all this working useth the office of a kind nurse that hath nought else to do but to give heed about the salvation of her child.

Juliana of Norwich

The Blessing of the Paschal Candle

Now let the angelic heavenly choirs exult; let joy pervade the unknown beings who surround God's throne; and let the trumpet of salvation sound the triumph of this mighty King. Let earth, too, be joyful, in the radiance of this great splendour. Enlightened by the glory of her Eternal King, let her feel that from the whole round world the darkness has been lifted. Let mother Church likewise rejoice, wearing the radiance of this great Light; let this temple echo with the multitude's full-throated song. . . .

Right indeed it is and just, with all the ardour of our heart and mind and with the service of our voice, to hymn God, the invisible almighty Father, and his only-begotten Son, our Lord Jesus Christ, who repaid Adam's debt for us to his eternal Father, and with his dear blood wiped out the penalty of that ancient sin. This is the paschal feast wherein is slain the true Lamb whose blood hallows the doorposts of the faithful. This is the night on which thou didst first cause our forefathers, the sons of Israel, in their

passage out of Egypt, to pass dry-shod over the Red Sea.
This is the night which purged away the blackness of sin
by the light of the fiery pillar. This is the night which at
this hour throughout the world restores to grace and yokes
to holiness those who believe in Christ, detaching them
from worldly vice and all the murk of sin. On this night
Christ burst the bonds of death and rose victorious from
the grave. Without redemption, life itself had been no
boon. How wonderful the condescension of thy mercy towards us; how far beyond all reckoning thy lovingkind-
ness! To ransom thy slave, thou gavest up thy Son! O truly
necessary sin of Adam, that Christ's death blotted out; and
happy fault, that merited such a Redeemer! Blessed indeed is this, the sole night counted worthy to know the
season and the hour in which Christ rose again from the
grave. It is this night of which the scripture says: And the
night shall be bright as day. And the night shall light up
my joy. By this night's holiness crime is banished, and sin
washed away; innocence is restored to the fallen, and gladness to the sorrowful. It drives forth hate, brings peace,
and humbles tyranny.

In thanksgiving for this night, then, holy Father, receive the evening sacrifice of this incense, which Holy
Church, by the hands of her ministers, renders to thee in
the solemn offering of this wax candle wrought by bees.
For now we see the splendour of this column, kindled to
the glory of God from shining flame.

A flame which though it be divided into parts, yet
suffers no loss of light, being fed from the ever-melting
wax that the mother-bee brought forth to form the substance of this precious candle.

Blessed indeed is the night, which despoiled the Egyptians and enriched the Hebrews! The night on which heaven is wedded to earth, the things of God to those of man! We, therefore, pray thee, Lord, that this candle, hallowed in honour of thy name, may continue unfailingly to scatter the darkness of this night. May it be received as a sweet fragrance, and mingle with the lights of heaven. May the morning-star find its flame alight, that Morning-Star which knows no setting, which came back from limbo and shed its clear light upon mankind. We pray thee, Lord, to grant us a season of peace at this time of Easter gladness. Deign to preserve us thy servants, and all the clergy and faithful people, together with our most blessed Pope and our Bishop. Guide and keep them all under thy continual protection: through the same Jesus Christ thy Son, our Lord, who is God, living and reigning with thee in the unity of the Holy Spirit for ever. Amen.

Roman Liturgy—
Holy Saturday Mass: Blessing of the Fire

IV
God in His Creation

Scattering a thousand graces,
He passed through these groves in haste,
And looking upon them as He went,
Left them, by His glance alone, clothed
with beauty.

St. John of the Cross

The Holiness of Created Things

A tree gives glory to God first of all by being a tree. For in being what God means it to be, it is imitating an idea which is in God and which is not distinct from the essence of God, and therefore a tree imitates God by being a tree.

The more it is like itself, the more it is like Him. If it tried to be like something else which it was never intended to be, it would be less like God and therefore it would give Him less glory.

But there is something more. No two trees are alike. And their individuality is no imperfection. On the contrary: the perfection of each created thing is not merely in its conformity to an abstract type but in its own individual identity with itself. This particular tree will give glory to God by spreading out its roots in the earth and raising its branches into the air and the light in a way that no other tree before or after it ever did or will do.

Do you imagine that all the individual created things in the world are imperfect attempts at reproducing an ideal type which the Creator never quite succeeded in actualizing on earth? If that is so they do not give Him glory but proclaim that He is not a perfect Creator.

Therefore each particular being, in its individuality, its concrete nature and entity, with all its own characteristics and its private qualities and its own inviolable identity, gives glory to God by being precisely what He wants it to be here and now, in the circumstances ordained for it by His Love and His infinite Art.

The forms and individual characters of living and growing things and of inanimate things and of animals and flowers and all nature, constitute their holiness in the sight of God.

Their inscape[1] is their sanctity. The special clumsy beauty of this particular colt on this April day in this field under these clouds is a holiness consecrated to God by His own Art, and it declares the glory of God.

The pale flowers of the dogwood outside this window are saints. The little yellow flowers that nobody notices on the edge of that road are saints looking up into the face of God.

This leaf has its own texture and its own pattern of veins and its own holy shape, and the bass and trout hiding in the deep pools of the river are canonized by their beauty and their strength.

But the great, gashed, half-naked mountain is another of God's saints. There is no other like it. It is alone in its own character; nothing else in the world ever did or ever will imitate God in quite the same way. And that is its sanctity.

Thomas Merton

---

[1] A word coined by Gerard Manley Hopkins. The meaning is that of distinctive quality, uniqueness—"the outward reflection of the inner nature of a thing" (cf. W. A. M. Peters, S.J., *Gerard Manley Hopkins: A Critical Essay towards the Understanding of His Poetry*, London and New York: Oxford University Press, 1948).

Behold God in All Things

He [St. Francis] exulted in all the works of the Lord's hands, and penetrated through those pleasant sights to their life-giving Cause and Principle. . . . When the brethren were cutting wood he forbad them to cut down a whole tree, so that it might have hope of sprouting again. He bade the gardener not dig up the outlying parts round the garden, in order that in their seasons the greenness of grass and the beauty of flowers might proclaim the beauteous Father of all things. In the garden he ordered a plot to be set apart for sweet-scented and flowering plants, that they might cause those that should look upon them to remember the Eternal Sweetness.

Thomas of Celano

A certain man, on seeing an unusually beautiful woman, praised the Creator. The sight of her enflamed his love for God, and tears rushed from his eyes. And it was wondrous to see how that which could for many have been a cause of sin turned for him, in a supernatural way, into a crown of victory. If such a man would on similar occasions act always in just this way, he would be incorruptible long before the general resurrection.

St. John Climacus

The Perpetual Miracle

The mark of holiness is to make us live in an atmosphere of perpetual miracle. We are in that atmosphere when we are conscious of the presence and action of God in all we see and do. . . . It is not true to say that the saint has turned his back on the world. On the contrary, he is the only one who has access to the deep life of the world, instead of remaining merely on the surface. Far from vanishing like a dream, the world reveals to him the deep foundations on which it rests. For him it reflects the face of God, while for those who look on it through bodily eyes alone it means nothing. To see the world thus transfigured is the privilege of those who, instead of thinking that our natural powers suffice to interpret the world to us, suffer a change of heart which makes them attentive to the presence of God; and from Him proceeds the power to greet all things with the glance of love.

Louis Lavelle

Praise to God

O burning Mountain, O chosen Sun,
O full Moon, O fathomless Well,
O unreachable Height, O Clarity beyond measure,
O Wisdom without ground, O Mercy without hindrance,
O Strength without resistance, O Crown of all glory,
The lowest of Thy creatures sings Thy praise.

Mechthild of Magdeburg

God's Grandeur

The world is charged with the grandeur of God.
  It will flame out, like shining from shook foil;
  It gathers to a greatness, like the ooze of oil
Crushed. Why do men then now not reck his rod?
Generations have trod, have trod, have trod;
  And all is seared with trade; bleared, smeared with toil;
  And wears man's smudge and shares man's smell; the soil
Is bare now, nor can foot feel, being shod.

And for all this, nature is never spent;
  There lives the dearest freshness deep down things;
And though the last lights off the black West went
  Oh, morning, at the brown brink eastward, springs—
Because the Holy Ghost over the bent
  World broods with warm breast and with ah! bright wings.

Gerard Manley Hopkins

How the Soul Finds God in All Creatures by Means of the Senses

O Love Divine and Great,
  Why dost thou still besiege my heart?
  Of me infatuate thou art,
  From me thou canst not rest!

My five engirdling battlements
  Are all besieged by Thee;
The Ear, the Eye, Taste, Smell, and Touch,
  By Love, mine Enemy:
    If I come forth I cannot flee,
      Nor hide me from Thy quest.

If I come forth by way of Sight,
  Love, Love is all around;
In radiance painted on the skies,
  In colour on the ground:
    They plead with me, in beauty drowned,
      To take Thee to my breast.

If I come forth by Hearing's gate,
  O what is this I hear?
What is this woven mist of sound
  That breaks upon mine ear?
    Here's no escape! Thy voice is clear,—
      'Tis Love, in music drest.

If I come forth by way of Taste,
  In savours Thou art set;
That Love Divine, Who craves for me,
  And snares me in His net,
    Prisons me close, and closer yet,
      To be His child and guest.

If I come forth by way of Smell,
  Thine odours sweet and fine
In every creature I perceive,
  And every one divine;
Thy spears they are, to make me Thine,
  They wound at Thy behest.

If I come forth by way of Touch,
  On every creature fair
In sacred awe I lay my hands,
    For Thou art sculptured there;
    T'were madness, Love, this way to dare
      Escape Thy sweet conquest.

O Love, why do I flee from Thee?
  Why should I fear to yield?
Because Thou wouldst re-make my heart,
  In fires of love annealed?
No more myself, in Thee concealed,
  And by Thy love possessed.

I, if I see another moved
  The downward step to make,
I am made partner of his loss,
  I suffer for his sake:
Whom, Love Unmeasured, dost *Thou* take
  To Thy compassion blest?

Lead me to Christ, Who died for me,
  Draw me from sea to shore:
And make me mourn in penitence
  The wounds and griefs He bore:
Why did He suffer pains so sore?
  That I might be at rest.

Jacopone da Todi

The Two Divine Lessons

All creatures speak to us; they speak to us of truth, but essentially of happiness. Fundamentally they are but a word of God addressed to our mind and will.

But what is it they present by speaking of happiness? Obviously a passing, incomplete, finite happiness. And yet it is the true, the eternal, the infinite and sublime happiness they are meant to teach us. God has granted them attraction and allurement to this end.

Their beauty, their sweetness and charm are entice-ments in order to draw us to love; their deficiencies, limi-tations, and thorns are the opposite forces, and throw us back on the love of the Highest Good by means of suffer-ing, sadness, and tears.

But who listens to the Two Lessons? Where are the souls that do not become trapped by the first and remain there? Where are the souls that lift themselves up to the second, to the fullness of the message? Where are the souls that find their way from disappointments and vanities to the love that is from above? In other words, which souls break through sensuousness and egoism to love and virtue? They are the ones with a sense for the divine, realizing God as Supreme Love and Goodness. This sense and this tendency toward the Infinite Good is (if not smothered) the force in the soul that struggles against the tendency of the moment, the divided and incomplete good; and as this tendency toward the Eternal comes from One higher than we, it can wage war against the narrow love of self. It is the spring on which the free will rests, which chooses between the two forces and remains indeed free, because it can turn the scale either way.

If the decision is made in favour of the Infinite by surrendering the enjoyment of the moment to God, then we speak of sacrifice.

It is sacrifice that translates the Two Divine Lessons into action, and accomplishes the transition from the finite happiness the creatures speak of to the infinite happiness as promised by God.

Alphonse Gratry

What Is It That I Love?

But what is it that I love when I love You? Not the beauty of any bodily thing, nor the order of seasons, nor the brightness of light that rejoices the eye, nor the sweet melodies of all songs, nor the sweet fragrance of flowers and ointments and spices: not manna nor honey, not the limbs that carnal love embraces. None of these things do I love in loving my God. Yet in a sense I do love light and melody and fragrance and food and embrace when I love my God—the light and the voice and the fragrance and the food and embrace in the soul, when that light shines upon my soul which no place can contain, that voice sounds which no time can take from me, I breathe that fragrance which no wind scatters, I eat the food which is not lessened by eating, and I lie in the embrace which satiety never comes to sunder.

This it is that I love, when I love my God.

St. Augustine

V

Self-Naughting

God expects but one thing of you, and that
is that you should come out of yourself in
so far as you are a created being and let
God be God in you.

Meister Eckhart

In order to become myself I must cease to
be what I always thought I wanted to be,
and in order to find myself I must go out of
myself, and in order to live I have to die.

Thomas Merton

Egredere

Disordered self-love is the root of evil. Virtue, merit, and salvation consist in the conquering of self-love with the support of God.

The victory over self-love is sacrifice.

Sacrifice is the free act of a loving and courageous will that consents to go out of itself in order to go toward God and find itself in God.

To go out of oneself and to stay there, that is the whole question, the whole history, the whole drama of moral life.

I understand this "going out of oneself" with regard to God and the community of souls and not with regard to sensual nature; for if one considers our sensual relations in their variety and passionateness with regard to outward things, one must say that moral life consists in withdrawing from them in order to find oneself, and to go out of oneself in order to find God.

"To go out of oneself," says Fénelon, "in order to enter into the infinity of God."

To this Bossuet adds a thought of wonderful depth, in which the law of life finds its highest expression: one must, if one has God in oneself, go out once more and leave God for God's sake, as St. François de Sales and St. John of the Cross have put it. Thus the general law of life, or the law of eternal progress, could be expressed in the threefold word which Bossuet takes as a motto for his eulogy on St. Benedict:

Egredere, egredere, egredere!—"Go out of yourself, more

and more; go higher, always higher!" Go out, go continually out of your present state, that you may find a still
higher one in the infinity of God. "Thus we are ordered
to make our way unceasingly, so that we are not allowed
to come to a standstill even at God."

That is what one might call the eternal and perpetual
sacrifice.

In regard to this Thomassin wrote: "Virtues are not
conditions of the soul resting in itself, but leaps of the soul
away from itself into God."

Let us explain this more thoroughly:

Love is either love of order, or disordered self-love. Disordered self-love is vice. Love of order, or order in love, is
virtue.

. . . The order which is God moves and penetrates us
through the emotions, it gives us a natural, instinctive,
necessary love of the highest good, and moreover illuminates us through reason.

It is for us to win an idea of this free state of love (the
love for the highest order) by perpetually demolishing our
self-love, under the double influence of emotion and light
and by using our reason and freedom. Everything depends
—in the words of Malebranche—on our infinite effort to
destroy self-love, or concupiscence, which continually renews itself in us.

But how can this happen? How can our self-love be
destroyed?

Malebranche answers with the whole theory of Christian
sacrifice, going into the moral of the Gospel and the meaning of the Cross. This Plato foreshadowed when he said:
"Philosophizing means learning to die." But now Truth
has become Flesh, historically visible and experimentally
manifest.

"One must die," wrote Malebranche, "in order to see God and to be united to Him; for no one can live and see Him, says the Holy Scripture. But actually one dies to the extent that one leaves the body, as one separates oneself from the world and silences one's senses, imagination, and passions, by which one is tied to the body and its surroundings.

"One dies to the body and to the world in so far as one withdraws into oneself, listens to Truth, agrees with its order, and obeys it. The Eternal Wisdom is hidden to the eyes of all the living. Those, however, who have died to the world and to self, who have crucified their flesh with its dissipating lusts, who are crucified with Jesus Christ and in whom the world is crucified—those, in a word, who have a pure heart and an unblemished imagination—are capable of contemplating Truth. . . .

"One must start and continue to sacrifice oneself and expect perfecting and reward from God only; for the life of the Christian on earth is a perpetual sacrifice, by which he offers without ceasing his body, his concupiscence, his self-love, for the love of order."

What one calls moral progress, that is to say, the means of transition from egoism, or disordered self-love, to love of order, or rather order in love—this progress one calls sacrifice. . . .

In what should this sacrifice now consist?

We find everything condensed in a short passage of Bossuet; we shall try to conceive its depth:

Bossuet explains the words of St. Augustine: "My will led me to where I did not will." He shows how the unbridled will in the end leads to self-stultification and destruction, by trying to please itself. In fact this is the end at which the unsacrificed will arrives: it destroys and

enslaves itself. Bossuet adds: "You walk into slavery on
the path of independence. Do the opposite: go the way of
obedience into freedom!"

"What indeed," he continues, "is the freedom of God's
children if not the widening and broadening of a heart
that has freed itself from the finite? Therefore go out of
yourself, cut through, pull away! Your will is finite. As
long as it is shut up, it is shut off. Do you want to be
free? Then free yourself, have no other will but God's."

This means: Moral progress or sacrifice of will does not
consist in destroying the will but in tearing down its bar-
riers; not in enslaving but in freeing it, not in narrowing
but in opening up . . . uniting it with the divine so that
it wills like God and with God, increasing in freedom the
more it is abandoned to Him. . . .

As is shown here, the true idea of sacrifice is the very
opposite of false mysticism, which tends toward annihila-
tion of the finite and individual and its capacities by having everything dissolved by God and disappear in the
infinite. Christian mysticism, on the other hand, seeks to
perfect, through union with God, every being prepared
by sacrifice; it wants the unlimited realization of the
finite and of the limited by its union with the infinite. . . .

Dying to be reborn! "Whosoever seeks to keep his soul
will lose it; and whoever loses it will help it to live." One
must die to one's selfish life to be reborn so that one can
say indeed: I live, yet not I, it is Christ who lives in me.

This is what Christians call transition from death to life,
from darkness to light. This is what Bossuet calls the freedom of God's children, which is nothing but the widening
and broadening of a heart detached from all that is finite.

How wide, how great is the life of such a free man who
sees and wills in God! In such a one is fulfilled the great
prayer: "Thy will be done on earth as it is in heaven!"

It is after this that all creatures travail who, according to St. Paul, await their redemption from the appearance of the children of God.

This is the obedience of God's children and the greatness of the sacrificed will.

Alphonse Gratry

True and Perfect Obedience

True and perfect obedience is a virtue above all virtues. No great work can be accomplished without it; nor can there be any task, however small or insignificant, which will not be done to better purpose in obedience, whether it be hearing or reading the Mass, or prayer, or contemplation, or whatever. Take any project you please, however trifling; it is improved and exalted by obedience. Obedience brings out the best of everything; it never fails or errs in any matter; and no matter what you do, if you do it in true obedience, it will not miss being good.

. . . Being obedient, if a man purifies himself, God will come into him in course; for when he has no will of his own, then God will command for him what God would command for himself. When I give my will up to the care of my prelate, and have no will of my own, God must will for me; for if he were to neglect me, he would be neglecting himself. So it is with everything: where I do not choose for myself, God chooses for me.

What will He choose for me? That I shall not choose for myself. When I deny myself, his will for me is identical with his will for himself, just as if it were for him alone; and if he did not so behave, then by the truth that God is, he would not be just, nor would he be what it is his nature to be. You will never hear an obedient person saying: "I want it so and so; I must have this or that." You will hear only of utter denial of self. Therefore, in the best prayer that man may offer, he will not say: "Give me virtue or a way," nor "Yea, Lord, give me thyself or life eternal," but only "Lord, give me nothing but what thou wilt and dost—Lord, what and how thou wilt in every detail!"

This exceeds the first prayer as heaven the earth; and when one has achieved it, he has prayed well. He has given up to God in true obedience, and just as there is no "I want this" in true obedience, so he will never be heard saying "I will not"; for "I will not" is the bane of obedience. According to St. Augustine, the true servant of God will not be pleased when someone gives him or says to him what he would like to see or hear; his first and chief care is what pleases God most.

The strongest prayer, one well-nigh almighty in what it can effect, and the most exalted work a man can do proceed from a pure heart. The more pure it is, the more powerful, and the more exalted, useful, laudable and perfect is its prayer and work. A pure heart is capable of anything.

What is a pure heart?

A pure heart is one that is unencumbered, unworried, uncommitted, and which does not want its own way about anything but which, rather, is submerged in the loving will of God, having denied self. Let a job be ever so inconsiderable, it will be raised in effectiveness and dimension by a pure heart.

We ought so to pray that every member and faculty,

eyes, ears, mouth, heart, and the senses shall be directed
to this end and never to cease prayer until we attain unity
with him to whom our prayers and attention are directed,
namely, God.

Meister Eckhart

Mortification and Non-attachment

One day the young Bishop of Belley asked François de
Sales: "Can you explain, my dear Father, how it is possible
for those who are themselves high in office to exercise the
virtue of obedience?"

He replied saying: ". . . There is no office so high which
does not have a spiritual superior to which it is subject in
matters concerning the conscience and the soul. We must
remember, however, that there is still a higher point of
obedience at which all superiors may aim. Does not St.
Paul refer to it when he says: 'For whereas I was free to
all, I made myself the servant to all, that I might gain the
more.' It is through this universal obedience to all men
that we become 'all things to all men.' And by serving
everyone for the sake of God, we regard all as our superiors."

Indeed, I have frequently noticed how the Bishop [St.
François] regarded everyone, even the most insignificant
person, as though he himself were the inferior. Never did
he turn anyone away; never did he refuse to converse or
listen to anyone. Nor did he ever betray the slightest sign
of weariness, impatience or annoyance no matter how in-
convenient the interruption may have been. His perennial
reply was: "It is God's will. It is what He asks of me in
this moment—what more do I need? While I am doing this

I am not required to do anything else! God's will is the center from which all we do must radiate. Everything else is mere excitement and frustration."

Jean Pierre Camus

St. Ignatius Loyola was once asked what his feelings would be if the Pope were to suppress the Company of Jesus. "A quarter of an hour of prayer," he answered, "and I should think no more about it."

From the life of St. Ignatius Loyola

One day Brother Yves saw an old woman crossing the street; in her right hand she was carrying a bowl full of fire, and in her left hand a jug of water. "What are you going to do with those?" Brother Yves asked her. She answered that with the fire she was going to burn Paradise, so that it should exist no more, and with the water extinguish Hell, so that there should be no more Hell. "And why," he asked, "do you wish to do that?" "Because I want no one ever to do good in order to have the reward of Paradise, or for fear of Hell, but only to have the love of God, who is so precious and can give us all that there is of goodness."

Jean de Joinville

How to Surrender the Will to God

My beloved children, look into your own self and see whatever is disordered therein, leave yourself and follow God on whatever path or way He wants to lead you: you will soon break through and take whatever comes from God, outwardly or inwardly, and accept His hidden judgements and trials with gratitude. Strange as they may seem at times, and uneven, in them you will be better dressed than in all the highest modes by which you believe to achieve the most exalted things.

You will say: "Oh Lord, I wish I had control over myself and inward peace like this or that person!" No, my child, it must be otherwise. First you must strip yourself, become aware of your nothingness, and see what lies hidden and covered up in you. Remain in yourself! . . .

But this you will not do and you look for everything outside and therefore will find neither God nor yourself; and such a course you will take for twenty years or more, leading what seems to be a spiritual life, and at the end you will have come just as near or just as far as you were on the first day. How pitiable such a life is! Therefore go and root out the weeds in you and not your nature! If you fail to do this, you lose in an hour what you have gathered in years with great pains. As long as you are possessed in your will by manifold modes and manners and you have dressed yourself in them, the Bridegroom cannot dress you in His own will. Mean and love only God and His honour from the bottom of your heart and do not seek for your own in anything, but give yourself a prisoner to the Divine Darkness, to the Unfathomableness of the hidden abyss, following wherever He leads you: then He will dress you with Himself blissfully, as "eyes hath not seen, nor ear heard, neither hath it entered into the heart of man."

Johannes Tauler

The Arduous Way

The way, however, is exceedingly arduous, so arduous, in fact, as to terrify all except the bravest of lovers. It comes to this, that we must surrender all that is dearest to us in the enjoyment of the senses and go through a dark night in which we live without their help and comfort. Then when this is accomplished we have to sacrifice the prerogative of our own way of thinking and willing and undergo another still darker night in which we have deprived ourselves of all the supports which are familiar to us and make us self-sufficient. This is a kind of death, the making nothing of all that we are to ourselves; but the genuine mystic tells us that when all has been strained away our emptiness will be filled with a new presence; our uncovered soul will receive the contact of divine love, and a new circuit of love will begin, when the soul is passive to an indescribable love which is given to it.

M. C. D'Arcy, S.J.[1]

[1] *The Poems of St. John of the Cross,* Preface.

What Sign Does the Beloved Bear
upon His Banner?

The Lover asked his Beloved if there remained in Him anything still to be loved. And the Beloved answered that he had still to love that by which his own love could be increased.

Said the Lover to the Beloved: 'Thou that fillest the sun with splendour, fill my heart with love.' The Beloved answered: 'Hadst thou not fullness of love, thine eyes had not shed those tears, neither hadst thou come to this place to see Him that loves thee.'

The birds hymned the dawn, and the Lover, who is the dawn, awakened. And the birds ended their song, and the Lover died in the dawn for his Beloved.

'O bird that singest of love, ask thou of my Beloved, Who has taken me to be His servant, wherefore He tortures me with love.' The bird replied: 'If Love made thee not to bear trials, wherewith couldst thou show thy love for him?'

The Lover wept, and sang songs of his Beloved, and said: 'Swifter is love in the heart of the lover than is the splendour of the lightning to the eye, or the thunder to the ear. The tears of love gather more swiftly than the waves of the sea; and sighing is more proper to love than is whiteness to snow.'

The Lover was all alone, in the shade of a fair tree. Men passed by that place, and asked him why he was alone. And the Lover answered: 'I am alone, now that I have seen you and heard you; until now, I was in the company of my Beloved.'

The Beloved revealed Himself to His Lover, clothed in new and scarlet robes. He stretched out His Arms to embrace him; He inclined His Head to kiss him; and He remained on high that he might ever seek Him.

They asked the Lover what sign his Beloved bore upon His banner. He answered: 'The sign of a Man that was dead.' They asked him why He bore such a sign. He answered: 'Because He became Man and died on a Cross, and because they that glory in being His lovers must follow in His steps.'

Love shone through the cloud which had come between the Lover and the Beloved, and made it to be as bright and resplendent as is the moon by night, as the day-star at dawn, as the sun at midday, and as the understanding in the will; and through that bright cloud the Lover and the Beloved held converse.

Said the Lover: 'O ye that love, if ye will have fire, come light your lanterns at my heart; if water, come to my eyes, whence flow the tears in streams; if thoughts of love, come gather them from my meditations.'

'Say, O Fool! what is solitude?' He answered: 'It is solace and companionship between Lover and Beloved.' 'And what are solace and companionship?' 'Solitude in the heart of the Lover,' he replied, 'when he remembers naught save only his Beloved.'

Ramón Lull

VI

About the Essence of God

*The first step to be taken by the soul who
enters upon the straight way and desires to
draw near to God, is to learn to know God
in very truth and not only outwardly as
though by the colour of the writing. For as
we know, so do we love: therefore if we
know but little and darkly, if we reflect and
meditate upon Him only superficially and
fleetingly, we shall in consequence love Him
but little.*

Angela of Foligno

*Who is God? I can think of no better an-
swer than, He who is. Nothing is more
appropriate to the eternity which God is.
If you call God good, or great, or blessed,
or wise, or anything else of this sort, it is
included in these words, namely, He is.*

St. Bernard of Clairvaux

*Why dost thou prate of God? Whatever
thou sayest of Him is untrue.*[1]

Meister Eckhart

[1] In this Meister Eckhart is not affirming that all theological state-
ments about God are false. He is merely following the *via negationis*
—meaning that all that we can say about God and His divine attributes remains insufficient.

Only Unspeakably It Is Seen

We are to believe of God in this wise, and as far as the Holy Spirit aideth we are to think of Him also in this wise: He is an everlasting life, living and life-giving, unchangeable, making all changeable things after an unchangeable manner, understanding, and creating every understanding and creature that understandeth, a wisdom making wise every creature that is wise, a truth that is fixed, that standeth fast and that turneth not aside, whereby all things are true that are true, and wherein the causes of all things that come to pass in time have an everlasting being. And to Him life is very essence and very nature; and He is a life living to Himself, very Divinity, eternity, greatness, goodness and virtue existing and subsisting in itself, passing beyond all place by virtue of His nature that knoweth no place, and by His eternity all time that may be comprehended, whether by reason or imagination: which is a far more true and surpassing thing than may be felt in any manner of feeling. Yet He is more surely attained by the feeling of humble enlightened love than by any conceiving of the reason, and is ever better than can be conceived; nevertheless He may be better conceived than spoken of. For He is the Sovereign Essence from which all being proceedeth; He is the Sovereign Substance that falleth under no predication of words; but the subsisting principle and cause of all things, wherein our being dieth not, our understanding erreth not, our love is offended not; Who is ever sought that He may the more sweetly be found, and most sweetly found that He may the more diligently be sought.

He therefore that would see this unspeakable (for only unspeakably it is seen), let him cleanse his heart; for by no bodily likeness to one sleeping, by no bodily vision to one waking, by no searching of the reason may it be seen or apprehended, but only by the clean heart of a humble lover. For this is the face of the Lord which no man may see and live to this world; this is the vision after which sigheth every creature that laboureth to love the Lord his God with all his heart, with all his soul, with all his mind and with all his might. Whereto he ceaseth not also to stir his neighbour, if he love him as himself. Whereunto if he is sometimes suffered to enter, in the very light of Truth he seeth past doubting the grace that runneth before; when he is cast out therefrom, in the midst of his blindness he seeth that his uncleanness may not be borne by that purity. And if he be a true lover, he thinketh it sweet to weep and not without much groaning is he compelled to return to the knowledge of himself. And though to conceive this unspeakable we be all unable, yet doeth our Beloved pardon us; for though we confess that of Him we may not worthily speak or think, yet to that speaking and that thinking we are stirred and drawn by the love of Him or love of the love of Him.

Wherefore it is part of him that thinketh, to humble himself in all things, to glorify in himself the Lord his God, to become as nought to himself in the contemplation of God, to be subject to every human creature for love of the Creator; to present his body as a living sacrifice, and above all things not to be more wise than he ought to be wise, but to be wise unto sobriety; and according to the measure of faith God giveth him not to show forth his good things before the face of man, but to hide them in his cell and to lay them up in his conscience; that both on his cell and on the forehead of his conscience he may have this title written:

My secret is to myself, my secret is to myself.

William of Saint Thierry

The Divine Essence

After the introduction of the outward into the inward man had taken place in a way conformable to right reason, high thoughts arose in the daughter's mind, and she inquired whether she might yet venture to ask questions about them. The Servitor replied:— Yes; if thou hast been duly led through the proper intermediate stages, it is quite lawful now for thy spiritual intelligence to ask about high things. Ask what thou wilt. She made answer:— Tell me what is God? and where is God? and how is God? I mean how He is single and yet three-fold?

The Servitor replied:— God knows, these are high questions. As to the first—what is God?—thou must know that all the learned doctors who ever were cannot fully explain it; for God is above all sense and reason. And yet a diligent man, by hard seeking, gains some knowledge of God, though in a very far-off way; and it is in this knowledge that man's supreme bliss consists. Thus it was that in days of old certain virtuous heathen doctors sought after God, especially the intellectual Aristotle. He pried minutely into the course of nature, in order to discover who he is who is Lord of nature. He searched after Him diligently, and found Him. He proved, from the well-ordered course of nature, that there must necessarily be one only prince and lord of all creatures, and that is what we mean by the name God.

Of this God and Lord we know thus much: That he is a substantial being; that he is everlasting, without before or after; that he is simple and unchangeable; an unembodied and essential Spirit; whose being is to live and work; whose essential reason knows all things in itself and by itself; whose being's fathomless delight is in itself; and who is to Himself, and to all who shall enjoy Him in the way of contemplation, a supernatural, unspeakable, and entrancing bliss.

The daughter looked upwards and said:— This is good to hear, for it stirs the heart and lifts the soul sursum, on high above itself. Therefore, dear father, tell me more about it.

He answered:— Behold, then. The divine essence, of which it is said that it is a rational substance, of such nature that no mortal eye can see it in itself, may nevertheless be discerned in its effects, just as we trace a good craftsman in his works. For, as St. Paul says, creatures are like a mirror which reflects God. And this mode of gaining knowledge we term reflection.

But let us pause here awhile, and reflect upon the high and venerable Master as mirrored in his works. Look above thee and around thee to the four quarters of the universe, and see how wide and high the beautiful heaven is in its swift course, and how nobly its Master has adorned it with the seven planets, each of which, not to reckon in the moon, is much bigger than the whole earth, and how He has decked it with the countless multitude of the bright stars. Oh! when in summer time the beautiful sun bursts forth unclouded and serene, what fruitfulness and blessings it bestows unceasingly upon the earth! See how the

leaves and grass shoot up, and the lovely flowers smile;
how forest, heath, and meadow ring again with the sweet
song of nightingales and other birds; how all those little
creatures, which stern winter had shut up, issue forth
rejoicing, and pair together; and how men too, both young
and old, entranced with joy, disport themselves right mer-
rily. Ah, gentle God, if Thou art so lovely in Thy creatures, how exceeding beautiful and ravishing Thou must
be in Thyself! But look again, I pray thee, and behold
the four elements—earth, water, air, and fire, with all the
wondrous things which they contain in manifold variety—
men, beasts, birds, fishes, and sea-monsters; and mark how
they all cry aloud together, Praise and honour be to the
unfathomable immensity that is in Thee! Who is it, Lord,
that sustains all this? Who feeds it all? It is Thou who
providest for all, each in its own way; for great and small,
for rich and poor. It is Thou, O God, who doest this.
Thou, O God, art God indeed!

The good daughter said:— Sir, I have now indeed found
out what God is; but I would fain know also where God
is. He answered:— Thou shalt hear this. The learned doctors say that God has no *where,* but that He is all in all.
Open the inward ears of thy soul and give good heed.
These same doctors tell us in the art of logic, that we come
to know what a thing is through its name. Now, one doctor says that being is the first name of God. Turn, then,
thine eyes to being in its pure and naked simplicity, and
take no note of this or that partial being. Consider only
being in itself, unmixed with all non-being. For as all non-
being is the negation of all-being, even so being in itself is
the negation of all non-being. A thing which has yet to be,
or which once was, is not now at this moment in actual
being. Moreover, we can have no knowledge of mixed

being or non-being, unless we take into account that which is all-being. For if we would understand what any thing is, the first point which our mind meets with in it is being, and this is a being which is the efficient cause of all things. It is not the partial and particular being of this or that creature; for partial being is always mixed with some other element, and has a capacity for receiving something new into it. Therefore, the nameless Divine Being must be in itself a being that is all-being, and that sustains all particular beings by its presence.

It is a proof of the singular blindness of man's reason, that it cannot examine into that which it contemplates first before everything, and without which it can not perceive any thing. It is with the reason as with the eye. When the eye is intent upon observing a variety of coloured objects, it does not notice the light which enables it to see all these objects, and even if it looks at the light, it still does not see it. Thus, too, it is with our soul's eye; when it looks at this or that particular being, it takes no heed of the being, which is everywhere one, absolute and simple, and which enables it to apprehend all other things. Hence a wise doctor says, that the eye of our intelligence, owing to its infirmity, is affected towards that being which is in itself the most manifest of all beings as the eye of a bat or a night-owl towards the bright light of the sun; for particular beings distract and dazzle the mind, so that it cannot see the Divine darkness, which is in itself the brightest of all brightness.

Open now thy inward eyes and gaze as best thou canst on being in its naked simple purity, and thou wilt see at once that it comes from no one, and has no before or after, and no capacity of change, either from within or from without, because it is a simple being. Thou wilt note, too, that it is the most actual, the most present, and the most perfect of all beings, without flaw or alteration, because it is absolutely one in naked simplicity. And this truth is so evident to an enlightened reason that it is impossible for it to think otherwise; for one point proves and implies the other. Thus, because it is a simple being, it must needs be the first of beings, and without origin and everlasting; and because it is the first and everlasting and simple, it must be the most present. It is at the very highest summit of perfection and simplicity, to which nothing can be added and from which nothing can be taken away. If thou canst understand what I have just told thee about the pure Godhead, thou wilt have been guided a long way into the incomprehensible light of God's hidden truth. This pure and simple being is the first and highest cause of all beings which have a cause (created beings), and by its peculiar presence it encloses, as the beginning and end of all things, whatever comes into being in time. It is altogether in all things, and altogether outside all things. Hence a certain doctor says:— God is a circular ring, whose centre is everywhere and circumference nowhere.

Heinrich Suso

A Parable of the Greatness of God

Humility is that lovely flower which, under the illuminating and warming rays of grace, grows forth from the knowledge of the divine greatness and our own lowness.

How much Aegidius was filled with the idea of God's greatness is shown by a discourse he had with two preaching friars. These travelled to Cetona to show their veneration and visited him. When they conversed with one another about God, one of them said: "Venerable Father, exceedingly great and lofty things have been said about God by the holy Evangelist John."

"Beloved Brother, St. John has said nothing about God."

"Beloved Father, take heed; what are you saying? St. Augustine tells us, had St. John spoken more loftily, no mortal would have understood him. Therefore, Father, tell us not that he said nothing."

"Again and again I tell you that St. John has said nothing about God."

Thereupon his visitors became indignant and, little pleased, prepared themselves to leave. After they had removed themselves a few paces, Aegidius called them back, and pointing to the mountain in back of Cetona, said: "If there existed a mountain of grain as high as this one, and a sparrow dwelling at its foot should eat from it: how much would he carry off in a day, a month, a year—nay, in a hundred years?"

"In a thousand years he would hardly carry off anything."

Now Aegidius continued: "The Eternal Godhead is so immeasurable and so high a mountain, that St. John, who was, as it were, a sparrow, said nought that could compare with the greatness of God."

As the two friars understood now that he had spoken truly, they flung themselves at his feet and after having asked for forgiveness and his prayers, went their way in an exalted spirit and filled with reverence.

From the life of Blessed Aegidius of Assisi

The Most High Attributes of God

The most high Nature of the Godhead may thus be perceived and beheld: how it is Simplicity and Onefoldness, inaccessible Height and bottomless Depth, incomprehensible Breadth and eternal Length, a dark Silence, a wild Desert, the Rest of all saints in the Unity, and a common Fruition of Himself and of all saints in Eternity. And many other marvels may be seen in the abysmal Sea of the Godhead; and though, because of the grossness of the senses to which they must be shown from without, we must use sensible images, yet, in truth, these things are perceived and beheld from within, as an abysmal and unconditioned Good. But if they must be shown from without, it must be done by means of diverse similitudes and images, according to the enlightenment of the reason of him who shapes and shows them.

The enlightened man shall also mark and behold the attributes of the Father in the Godhead: how He is omnipotent Power and Might, Creator, Mover, Preserver, Beginning and End, the Origin and Being of all creatures. This the rill of grace shows to the enlightened reason in its radiance. It also shows the attributes of the Eternal Word: abysmal Wisdom and Truth, Pattern of all creatures and all life, Eternal and unchanging Rule, Seeing all things and Seeing Through all things, none of which is hidden from Him; Transillumination and Enlightenment of all saints in heaven and on earth, according to the merits of each. And even as this rill of radiance shows the distinctions between many things, so it also shows to the enlightened reason the attributes of the Holy Ghost: incomprehensible Love and Generosity, Compassion and Mercy, infinite Faithfulness and Benevolence, inconceivable Greatness, outpouring Richness, a limitless Goodness drenching through all heavenly spirits with delight, a Flame of Fire which burns all things together in the Unity, a flowing Fountain, rich in all savours, according to the desire of each; the Preparation of all saints for their eternal bliss and their entrance therein, an Embrace and Penetration of the Father, the Son, and all saints in fruitive Unity. All this is observed and beheld without differentiation or division in the simple Nature of the Godhead. And according to our perception these attributes abide as Persons do, in manifold distinctions. For between might and goodness, between generosity and truth, there are, according to our perception, great differences. Nevertheless all these are found in oneness and undifferentiation in the most high Nature of the Godhead. But the relations which make the personal attributes remain in eternal distinction. For the Father begets distinction. For the Father incessantly begets his Son, and Himself is unbegotten; and the Son is begotten, and cannot beget; and thus throughout eternity the Father has a Son, and the Son a Father. And these are the relations of the Father to the Son, and of the Son to the Father. And the Father and the Son breathe forth one Spirit, Who is Their common Will or Love. And this Spirit begets not, nor is He begotten; but must eternally pour forth, being breathed forth from both the Father and the Son. And these three Persons are one God and one Spirit. And all the attributes with the works which flow forth from them are common to all the Persons, for They work by virtue of Their Onefold Nature.

Jan van Ruysbroeck

The Darkness beyond Being

Trinity, exceeding all being, Godhead and Goodness! Thou that revealest divine wisdom! Lead us to the utmost height of mystic love, which exceedeth both light and knowledge, where the simple, absolute, and immutable mysteries of divine truth lie hidden in the dazzling darkness of that silence which revealeth in secret. For this darkness, though intense, outshines all brilliance; and though beyond all touch and sight, it more than fills our blinded minds with splendours of exceeding beauty. . . .

We pray to dwell in this dazzling darkness, and through not seeing and not knowing, to see and know Him who is beyond vision and knowledge. For this is indeed to see and to know and through the abandonment of all things to praise Him who is above and beyond all things.

For this is like the art of those who carve a natural image from stone, removing from around it all that prevents the pure vision of the veiled form, revealing its hidden beauty solely by taking away.

For it is, I believe, more fitting to praise Him by taking away than by affirming. For we affirm things of Him when we begin with universals and descend through the intermediate to the particulars. But here we take away all things from Him, ascending from particulars to universals, so that we may know openly the unknowable, which is veiled in and under all things that may be known.

And we behold the darkness beyond being, hidden under all natural light.

Dionysius the Areopagite[1]

---

[1] *De mystica theologia.*

VII
The Cloud of Unknowing

Up then, noble soul! Put on thy jumping shoes, which are intellect and love, and overleap the worship of thy mental powers, overleap thine understanding and spring into the heart of God, into the hiddenness where thou art hidden from all creatures.

Meister Eckhart

The Wisdom That Is Ignorance

Lift up thine heart unto God with a meek stirring of love; and mean himself and none of his goods. And thereto look that thou loathe to think on aught but himself, so that nought work in thy mind nor in thy will but only himself. And do that in thee is to forget all the creatures that ever God made and the works of them, so that thy thought or thy desire be not directed or stretched to any of them, neither in general nor in special. But let them be, with a seemly recklessness, and take no heed of them.

This is the work of the soul that most pleaseth God. All saints and angels have joy of this work and hasten them to help it with all their might. All fiends be mad when thou dost thus, and try for to defeat it in all that they can. All men living on earth be wonderfully helped by this work, thou knowest not how. Yea, the souls in purgatory are eased of their pains by virtue of this work. Thou thyself art cleansed and made virtuous by no work so much. And yet it is the lightest work of all, when a soul is helped with grace in sensible list; and soonest done. But else it is hard and wonderful for thee to do.

Cease not, therefore, but travail therein till thou feel list. For at the first time when thou dost it, thou findest but a darkness, and as it were a *cloud of unknowing*, thou knowest not what, saving that thou feelest in thy will a naked intent unto God. This darkness and this cloud, howsoever thou dost, is betwixt thee and thy God, and hindreth thee, so that thou mayest neither see him clearly by light of understanding in thy reason, nor feel him in sweetness of love in thine affection. And therefore shape thee to bide in this darkness as long as thou mayest, evermore crying after him whom thou lovest. For if ever thou shalt see him or feel him, as it may be here, it must always be in this cloud and in this darkness. And if thou wilt busily travail as I bid thee, I trust in his mercy that thou shalt come thereto. . . .

And therefore travail fast awhile, and beat upon this high *cloud of unknowing,* and rest afterwards. Nevertheless a travail shall he have, whoso shall use him in this work; yea, surely! and that a full great travail, unless he have a more special grace, or else he have for long time used him therein.

But I pray thee, wherein shall that travail be? Surely not in that devout stirring of love that is continually wrought in his will, not by himself, but by the hand of Almighty God, who is evermore ready to work this work in every soul that is disposed thereto, and that doth what in him is, and hath done long time before, to enable him to this work.

But wherein then is this travail, I pray thee? Surely, this travail is all in treading down of the thought of all the creatures that ever God made, and in holding of them under the *cloud of forgetting* named before. In this is all the travail; for this is man's travail, with the help of grace. And the other above—that is to say, the stirring of love— that is the work of only God. And therefore do on thy work, and surely I promise thee he shall not fail in his.

Do on then fast; let me see how thou bearest thee. Seest thou not how he standeth and abideth thee? For shame! Travail fast but awhile, and thou shalt soon be eased of the greatness and of the hardness of this travail. For although it be hard and strait in the beginning, when thou hast no devotion, nevertheless afterwards, when thou hast devotion, it shall be made full restful and full light unto thee, that before was full hard. And thou shalt have either little travail or none; for then will God work sometimes all by himself. But not always, nor yet a long time together, but when he liketh and as he liketh; and then wilt thou think it merry to let him alone.

Then will he sometimes peradventure send out a beam of ghostly light, piercing this *cloud of unknowing* that is betwixt thee and him, and show thee some of his secrets, the which man may not and cannot speak. Then shalt thou feel thine affection inflamed with the fire of his love, far more than I can tell thee, or may or will at this time. For of that work that pertaineth only to God dare I not take upon me to speak with my blabbering fleshly tongue: and, shortly to say, although I durst I would not.

The Cloud of Unknowing

Of Seeing Face to Face

In all faces is seen the Face of faces, veiled, and in a riddle; howbeit unveiled it is not seen, until above all faces a man enter into a certain secret and mystic silence where there is no knowledge or concept of a face. This mist, cloud, darkness or ignorance into which he that seeketh Thy face entereth when he goeth beyond all knowledge or concept, is the state below which Thy face cannot be found except veiled; but that very darkness revealeth Thy face to be there, beyond all veils. It is as when our eye seeketh to look on the light of the sun which is its face; first it beholdeth it veiled in the stars, and in colours and in all things that share its light. But when it striveth to behold the light unveiled, it goeth beyond all visible light, because all this is less than that which it seeketh. A man seeking to see a light beyond his seeing knoweth that, so long as he seeth aught, it is not that which he seeketh. Wherefore it behoveth him to go beyond all visible light. For him, then, who must go beyond all light, the place he entereth must needs lack visible light, and is thus, so to speak, darkness to the eye. And while he is in that darkness which is a mist, if he then know himself to be in a mist, he knoweth that he hath drawn nigh the face of the sun; for that mist in his eye proceedeth from the exceeding bright shining of the sun. Wherefore, the denser he knoweth the mist to be, by so much the more truly doth he attain in the mist unto the light invisible. I perceive that it is thus and not otherwise, Lord, that the light inaccessible, the beauty and radiance of Thy face, may, unveiled, be approached.

Nicholas of Cusa

Verses Written after an Ecstasy
of High Exaltation

I entered in, I know not where,
And I remained, though knowing naught,
Transcending knowledge with my thought.

Of when I entered I know naught,
But when I saw that I was there
(Though where it was I did not care)
Strange things I learned, with greatness fraught.
Yet what I heard I'll not declare.
But there I stayed, though knowing naught,
Transcending knowledge with my thought.

Of peace and piety interwound
This perfect science had been wrought,
Within the solitude profound
A straight and narrow path it taught,
Such secret wisdom there I found
That there I stammered, saying naught,
But topped all knowledge with my thought.

So borne aloft, so drunken-reeling,
So rapt was I, so swept away,
Within the scope of sense or feeling
My sense or feeling could not say.
And in my soul I felt, revealing,
A sense that, though its sense was naught,
Transcended knowledge with my thought.

The man who truly there has come
Of his own self must shed the guise;
Of all he knew before the sum
Seems far beneath that wondrous prize:
And in this lore he grows so wise
That he remains, though knowing naught,
Transcending knowledge with his thought.

The farther that I climbed the height
The less I seemed to understand
The cloud so tenebrous and grand
That there illuminates the night.
For he who understands that sight
Remains for aye, though knowing naught,
Transcending knowledge with his thought.

This wisdom without understanding
Is of so absolute a force
No wise man of whatever standing
Can ever stand against its course,
Unless they tap its wondrous source,
To know so much, though knowing naught,
They pass all knowledge with their thought.

This summit all so steeply towers
And is of excellence so high
No human faculties or powers
Can ever to the top come nigh.
Whoever with its steep could vie,
Though knowing nothing, would transcend
All thought, forever, without end.

If you would ask, what is its essence—
This summit of all sense and knowing:
It comes from the Divinest Presence—
The sudden sense of Him outflowing,
In His great clemency bestowing
The gift that leaves men knowing naught,
Yet passing knowledge with their thought.

St. John of the Cross[1]

[1] *The Poems of St. John of the Cross.*

Of the Love That Is Silent

Love, silent as the night,
  Who not one word wilt say,
That none may know thee right!

O love that lies concealed,
  Through heat and storm and cold,
That none may guess nor read
  Thy secrets manifold;
  Lest thieves should soon grow bold
    To steal away thy treasure,
    Snatch it and take to flight!

Deep-hid, thy secret fires
  More ardently shall glow;
And he who screens thee close,
  Thy fiercest heat shall know;
  But he who fain would show
    Thy mysteries, will be wounded,
    Scorched by thy fiery might.

The man who strives to tell
  That secret joy within,
In vain he babbles thus:—
  Before his words begin
  The bitter winds of sin
    Will storm and whirl around him,
    And wreck his treasure bright.

The man who sets his torch
  High on a candlestick,
To let it shine in peace,
  Shields it with shutters thick,
  Lest winds should catch the wick,
    —Through open casements blowing—
    And quench its flick'ring light.

'Tis Silence, at thy door
  Holds captive all thy sighs:
Mute Love hath set him there,
  He will not let him rise;
  So shalt thou hold thy prize
    That it may live within thee,
    Not scattered left and right.

For if thy sighs come forth,
  Therewith comes forth thy mind,
To wander far from home,
  And leave her joy behind,
  Nor can she ever find
    The Good, bestowed upon her,
    That Treasure Infinite.

Mute Love hath thrust away
  False Seeming from his side,
In Love's fair land and realm
  No longer to abide.
  Hypocrisy and Pride,
    And all that do them homage
    Are chased to outer night.

Jacopone da Todi

VIII
Ex Plenitudine Contemplationis

*The coin in your hand you may be able to
keep, but what rests in your soul is lost unless you spend it.*

Spanish proverb

*What a man takes in by contemplation,
that he pours out in love.*

Meister Eckhart

*The love of truth seeks holy leisure; the
necessity of love takes righteous action.*

St. Augustine

Mary and Martha

God is not a destroyer of nature but rather one who fulfills it, and he does this more and more as you are prepared.

You may, however, say: Alas, good man, if, to be prepared for God, one needs a heart freed from ideas and
activities which are natural to the agents of the soul, how
about those deeds of love which are wholly external, such
as teaching and comforting those who are in need? Are
these to be denied? Are we to forgo the deeds that occupied the disciples of our Lord so incessantly, the work
that occupied St. Paul on behalf of the people, so much
that he was like a father to them? Shall we be denied the
[divine] goodness because we do virtuous deeds?

Let us see how this question is to be answered. The one
[contemplation] is good. The other [deeds of virtue] is
necessary. Mary was praised for having chosen the better
part but Martha's life was useful, for she waited on Christ
and his disciples. St. Thomas [Aquinas] says that the active
life is better than the contemplative, for in it one pours
out the love he has received in contemplation. Yet it is
all one; for what we plant in the soil of contemplation we
shall reap in the harvest of action and thus the purpose
of contemplation is achieved. There is a transition from
one to the other but it is all a single process with one end
in view—that God is, after which it returns to what it was
before. If I go from one end of this house to the other, it
is true, I shall be moving and yet it will be all one motion.
In all he does, man has only his one vision of God. One is

based on the other and fulfills it. In the unity [one beholds] in contemplation, God foreshadows [variety of] the harvest of action. In contemplation, you serve only yourself. In good works, you serve many people.

The whole life of Christ instructs us in this matter, and the lives of his saints as well, all of whom he sent out into the world to teach the Many the one truth. St. Paul said to Timothy: "Beloved, preach the word!" Did he mean the audible word that beats the air? Certainly not! He referred to the inborn, secret word that lies hidden in the soul. It was this that he preached, so that it might instruct the faculties of people and nourish them, and so that the behavior of men might proclaim it and so that one might be fully prepared to serve the need of his neighbor. It should be in the thoughts, the mind, and the will. It should shine through your deeds. As Christ said: "Let your light so shine before men! . . . The tree that does not bear fruit . . . shall be hewn down."

Meister Eckhart

Action and Contemplation

Speaking of those who prefer immediate action to acquiring, through contemplation, the power to act well, St. John of the Cross asks, "What do they accomplish?"

And he answers: "Little more than nothing, and sometimes nothing at all, and sometimes even harm."

From the life of St. John of the Cross[1]

[1] Huxley, *The Perennial Philosophy.*

St. Vincent de Paul frequently admonished the Daughters of Charity to love prayer as the body loves the soul. The soul it is that gives life to the body, that gives motion to it, that enables it to speak and to act. And as the body cannot live without the soul, so the soul cannot live without prayer. And if a Daughter prays as she ought to pray, she will not walk, she will run in the ways of the Lord.

From the life of St. Vincent de Paul

I have often said that a person who wishes to begin a good life should be like a man who draws a circle. Let him get the center in the right place and keep it so and the circumference will be good. In other words, let a man first learn to fix his heart on God and then his good deeds will have virtue; but if a man's heart is unsteady, even the great things he does will be of small advantage.

No person in this life may reach the point at which he can be excused from outward service. Even if he is given to a life of contemplation, still he cannot refrain from going out and taking an active part in life. Even as a person who has nothing at all may still be generous for his will to give, another may have great wealth and not be generous because he gives nothing; so no man may have virtues without using them as time and occasion require. Thus, those who are given to the life of contemplation and avoid activities deceive themselves and are on the wrong track. I say that the contemplative person should indeed avoid even the thought of deeds to be done during the period of his contemplation but afterwards he should get busy, for no one can or should engage in contemplation all the time, for active life is to be a respite from contemplation.

Meister Eckhart

How the Contemplative Descends from the Heights
of Contemplation to the Needs of Christendom

St. Augustine says the soul has a hidden abyss, untouched
by time and world and far superior to anything that gives
life and movement to the body. In this noble and blissful
abyss, in this heavenly realm, there the soul has its eternal
ground.

There a man becomes silent and essential, single-minded
and detached, raised up in greater clearness and purity
and more and more removed from things, for God Himself is present in this noble realm, and works and lives and
governs there.

Such a man is not comparable to what he was before,
for now he partakes in the divine life, and his spirit melts
and enflames itself in all things, and is drawn into the
hot fire of love, which is God Himself in substance and
nature.

And from this height such men descend again into all
the needs of Christendom, and in holy prayer and desire
they turn to everything God wishes to be prayed for, and
to their friends. And they go toward the sinners and into
purgatory, wholly intent on serving in charity every man's
need—not praying for each person's selfish wishes, but
including the whole of Christendom in a simple, wise
manner.

Just as I see you all sitting before me at one glance, just
so they draw all into the same abyss, into the same fire
of love, in a ghostly manner; and after this they look again

into the abyss of love, into the fire of love, and there they
rest; and after plunging into it they descend to all that
are in want until they return to the loving, dark, silent
rest of the abyss.

Thus they go in and out and yet remain at all times
within, in the ground where their substance is and their
life, all their working and moving.

Wherever one finds such men one finds nothing but
divine life. Their conduct, their deeds, their manner are
from God. They are noble men, and the whole of Christendom draws profit from them. To all men they give
benefit, to God glory, and to all things comfort.

They live in God, and God in them. Where they are
they should be praised.

Johannes Tauler

The Inward Life According to Justice

God comes to us without ceasing, both with means and
without means, and demands of us both action and fruition, in such a way that the one never impedes, but always
strengthens, the other. And therefore the most inward
man lives his life in these two ways: namely, in work and
in rest.

And in each he is whole and undivided; for he is wholly
in God because he rests in fruition, and he is wholly in
himself because he loves in activity: and he is perpetually
called and urged by God to renew both the rest and the
work. And the justice of the spirit desires to pay every
hour that which is demanded of it by God. And therefore,
at each irradiation of God, the spirit turns inward, in

action and fruition; and thus it is renewed in every virtue, and is more deeply immersed in fruitive rest. For God gives, in one gift, Himself and His gifts; and the spirit gives, at each introversion, itself and all its works. For by means of the simple irradiation of God and the fruitive tendency and melting away of love, the spirit has been united with God, and is incessantly transported into rest. And through the gifts of Understanding and Savouring Wisdom, it is touched in an active way, and perpetually enlightened and enkindled in love. And there is shown and presented to it in the spirit all that one may desire. It is hungry and thirsty, for it beholds the food of the angels and the heavenly drink. It works diligently in love, for it beholds its rest. It is a pilgrim; and it sees its country. In love it strives for victory; for it sees its crown. Consolation, peace, joy, beauty and riches, and all that can delight it, are shown without measure in ghostly images to the reason which is enlightened in God. And through this showing and the touch of God, love remains active. For this just man has established a true life in the spirit, in rest and in work, which shall endure eternally; but, after this life, it shall be changed into a higher state. Thus the man is just; and he goes *towards* God with fervent love in eternal activity; and he goes *in* God with fruitive inclination in eternal rest. And he dwells in God, and yet goes forth towards all creatures in universal love, in virtue, and in justice. And this is the supreme summit of the inward life. All those men who do not possess both rest and work in one and the same exercise, have not yet attained this justice. This just man cannot be hindered in his introversion, for he turns inward both in fruition and in work; but he is like to a double mirror, which receives images on both sides. For in his higher part, the man receives

God with all His gifts; and in his lower part, he receives
bodily images through the senses. Now he can enter into
himself at will, and can practise justice without hindrance.
But man is unstable in this life, and that is why he often
turns outwards, and works in the senses, without need and
without the command of the enlightened reason; and thus
he falls into venial sins. But in the loving introversion of
the just man all venial sins are like to drops of water in
a glowing furnace.

Jan van Ruysbroeck

IX
Union

Let us rejoice, Beloved,
And let us go to see ourselves in Thy beauty,
To the mountain or the hill
Where flows the pure water . . .

St. John of the Cross

Song of the Soul in Rapture

Upon a gloomy night,
With all my cares to loving ardours flushed,
(O venture of delight!)
With nobody in sight
I went abroad when all my house was hushed.

In safety, in disguise,
In darkness up the secret stair I crept,
(O happy enterprise)
Concealed from other eyes
When all my house at length in silence slept.

Upon that lucky night
In secrecy, inscrutable to sight,
I went without discerning
And with no other light
Except for that which in my heart was burning.

It lit and led me through
More certain than the light of noonday clear
To where One waited near
Whose presence well I knew,
There where no other presence might appear.

Oh night that was my guide!
Oh darkness dearer than the morning's pride,
Oh night that joined the lover
To the beloved bride
Transfiguring them each into the other.

Within my flowering breast
Which only for himself entire I save
He sank into his rest
And all my gifts I gave
Lulled by the airs with which the cedars wave.

Over the ramparts fanned
While the fresh wind was fluttering his tresses,
With his serenest hand
My neck he wounded, and
Suspended every sense with its caresses.

Lost to myself I stayed
My face upon my lover having laid
From all endeavour ceasing:
And all my cares releasing
Threw them amongst the lilies there to fade.

St. John of the Cross[1]

[1] *The Poems of St. John of the Cross.*

Marriage to the Word

*In my bed by night I sought Him Whom my soul loveth:
I sought Him and found Him not.*

*I will rise, and will go about the city: in the streets and
the broad ways.*

*I will seek Him Whom my soul loveth: I sought Him
and found Him not.*

*The watchmen who keep the city, found me: Have you
seen Him Whom my soul loveth?*

When I had a little passed by them, I found Him
Whom my soul loveth: I held Him: and I will not let Him
go, till I bring Him into my mother's house, and into the
chamber of her that bore me.

We have learned that every soul, although weighed
down with sins, caught in the meshes of imperfections,
held captive in exile, imprisoned in the flesh, sunk in
mire, held fast in mud, fastened to the body, rendered
helpless by anxieties, distressed by business considerations,
grown suspicious because of fear, broken by sorrow, wan-
dering about in the midst of errors, worried by cares,
grown restless because of suspicions, and finally a stranger
in the land of enemies, and according to the word of the
Prophet, "defiled with the dead, . . . counted with them
that go down into hell"—although, I say, thus condemned
and thus despairing, we have learned that nevertheless this
soul can discover within herself not only the source
whence she can breathe again in the hope of forgiveness,
in the hope of mercy, but the source, as well, whence she
may dare to aspire to the nuptials of the Word, not fearing
to enter into an alliance of friendship with God Himself,
nor afraid to draw the sweet yoke of love with Him Who
is King of Angels. For what is there that she may not safely
dare in the presence of Him Whose image, she discerns,
gives her her distinction, and a likeness to Whom, she
knows, makes her noble. What terror, I say, has Majesty for
her to whom confidence is given by virtue of her very origin?
It is necessary only that she take care to preserve by an
upright life the purity of the nature given her at birth.
Rather, let her strive to increase that heavenly beauty
which is her birthright, and to adorn it with such shades
of character and affection as it deserves.

What, then, is the reason why she is so sluggish in action? Activity is assuredly a great gift of nature in us. And if it fails to perform its functions, will not the rest of our nature be completely thrown into disorder, and be entirely covered over with rust of long standing? This certainly would be an injustice to the Creator. And indeed the Creator, God Himself, wished to preserve perpetually in the soul the distinction of divine generosity, so that she might always have within herself those attributes received from the Word by which she would ever be reminded either to remain with the Word, or to return to Him if ever she should be removed from Him. She is not removed from Him in passing from one place to another, or in walking on her feet. But she is removed (as a spiritual substance can be removed) by her affections. Rather, by her defects she falls from her high estate, as it were, when she renders herself unlike her natural self by the depravity of her life and character, and becomes degenerate. This unlikeness, however, is not the destruction of nature, but it is a vice exalting the good of nature by contrast with itself. To the same degree it defiles the good by conjunction with it. Again, the return of the soul is her conversion to the Word, to be reformed through Him and to be made conformed to Him. In what respect? In charity. For it is said: "Be ye therefore followers of God, as most dear children. And walk in love, as Christ also hath loved us."

Such conformity joins the soul in marriage to the Word, when, being already like unto Him in nature, she shows herself no less like unto Him in will, loving as she is loved. If, then, she loves perfectly, she has become His bride. What is more delightful than this conformity? What is more to be desired than charity? From it, it follows that not content with human guidance, O soul, in your own person you confidently draw near to the Word, you cleave to the Word consistently, on terms of familiarity you ask questions of the Word and consult Him about every thing, your capacity of mind being measured only by the fearlessness of your desires. Truly spiritual and a contract of holy marriage is such a relationship as this. It is an understatement to call it a contract. It is an embrace—an embrace, surely, where to will and not to will the same thing, makes one spirit out of two. Nor should there be any fear that the inequality of the parties should make an agreement of wills defective in any way, because love knows no reverential fear. It is from loving, not from showing respect, that love takes its name. By all means, let him show honor who trembles and stands aghast with fear, who is filled with apprehension, who is struck with awe. But all these have no place in the case of one who loves. Love more than suffices for itself. Love, when it comes to a soul, converts everything else into itself and takes the affections captive. The soul, therefore, who loves, loves, and knows nothing else. He Himself Who is worthy of honor, Who is rightly the object of fear and of awe, nevertheless, loves still more, to be loved. They are Bridegroom and bride. What other relationship do you seek between a bride and bridegroom, except to be loved and to love. This union dissolves even what nature has fashioned rather firmly, the bond between parents and children. "For this cause," it is said, "shall a man leave father and mother, and shall cleave to his wife."

Add to this, that this Bridegroom is not only loving, but He is love. Is He not Honor? Let who will, maintain that He is. I, for one, have never read it. But I have read, "God is Charity." And I have not read that He is Honor or Dignity. Not that God does not desire honor—He who says: "If then I be a Father, where is my honor?" That He says as a Father. But if He presents Himself as a Bridegroom, I think that He will change what He has said, and say: "If I am a Bridegroom, where is my love?" For previously He has spoken thus: "If I be a Master, where is my fear?" It is fitting, therefore, that God be feared as Lord, be honored as Father, and that as Bridegroom He be loved. What one of these is best? What one stands out? Love, surely. Without this, both "fear hath pain," and honor has no charm. Fear is servile so long as it is not emancipated by love. And honor which does not spring from love, is not honor but flattery. And indeed it is to God alone that honor and glory are due, but neither of these will God accept, unless they have been sweetened with the honey of love. Love is sufficient of itself. Of itself it pleases and for its own sake. It is itself its own merit and its own reward. It seeks no motive, no fruit beyond itself. It is its own fruit, its own enjoyment. I love because I love. I love in order that I may love. Love is a great thing if only it returns to its First Principle, if it has been restored to its Source, if having flowed back to its Fountain-head, it draws from thence the power to flow on forever. Out of all the motions of the soul, those of the senses as well as those of the affections, it is love alone in which the creature can make a return to the Creator, although not on equal terms. For example, if God were angry with me, could I, in like manner, grow angry with Him in return? Certainly not. But I shall tremble and shake with fear, and pray forgiveness. Likewise if He rebukes me I shall not rebuke Him in return, but I shall justify Him. And if He condemns me I shall not condemn Him, but I shall adore Him. . . . If He exercises His power as my Lord and Master, I must act as His servant. If He commands, I must obey. . . . And now you must see how different it is in the case of love. For when God loves, He desires nothing else than to be loved. In fact, He loves for no other reason except that He may be loved, knowing that those who love Him have attained happiness by that very love itself.

Love is a great thing, but there are degrees in it. A bridegroom abides in the highest. For children also love, but they keep their inheritance in mind. And while they are afraid that they may, in some way or other, lose it, they show him from whom they expect the inheritance, more respect than love. . . . The one inheritance and hope of a bride is love. In this the bride abounds. With this the bridegroom is content. He seeks nothing else. And she possesses nothing else. It is for this reason that he is a bridegroom and she is a bride. It is the prerogative of those who are wed, to which no one else can attain, not even a son. . . . But the love of the Bridegroom, rather, the Bridegroom who is Love, asks only a return of love, and fidelity. Let the bride, therefore, return love for love.

With good reason renouncing all other affections the bride gives herself wholly to love alone—she who in reciprocating love is constrained to make a return of love to Him who is Love itself. For when she has poured out her whole being in love, what is this in comparison with the unceasing flow of the Fountain of Love? The waters of love do not flow with equal copiousness from the lover and from Him who is Love, from the bride and the Bridegroom, from the Creator and the creature. You might as well compare one who is thirsty and the fountain from which he drinks. What then? Will the hope of future nuptials cease on this account and become entirely void, together with the aspirations of one who sighs with longing, the ardor of one who loves, the trust of one who abounds in confidence, simply because she is unable to compete with a giant in a race, to rival honey in sweetness, a lamb in gentleness, a lily in radiant whiteness, the sun in brightness, and, in charity, Him who is Charity itself?

Assuredly not. For although a creature loves less because he is less, yet if he loves with his whole being, there can be nothing wanting. Hence, as I have said, to love thus is to have been joined in marriage with God, for it is impossible for the soul to love thus and to be imperfectly loved in return. And in the mutual consent of the two parties consists the integrity and perfection of marriage. But perhaps someone may doubt that the soul is first loved by the Word, and is more loved by Him. In very truth she is anticipated by Him in loving, and surpassed. Happy the soul who has deserved to be anticipated in the matter of a blessing so sweet. Happy the soul to whom it is given to experience an embrace of such intense delight. This is nothing else than love holy and chaste, love full of delight and sweet, love as untroubled as it is sincere, love that is mutual, intimate and strong, love which joins two together not in one flesh, but in one spirit, and makes these two no longer two, but one. As Saint Paul says: "He who is joined to the Lord, is one spirit."

Saint Bernard of Clairvaux

How One Enters into the God-seeing Life

Contemplation sets us in purity and clearness above all our understanding, for it is a singular adornment and a heavenly crown, and besides the eternal reward of all virtues and of our whole life. And to it none can attain through knowledge and subtlety, neither through any exercise whatsoever. Only he with whom it pleases God to be united in His Spirit, and whom it pleases Him to enlighten by Himself, can see God, and no one else. The mysterious Divine Nature is eternally and actively behold-ing and loving according to the Persons, and has everlast-ing fruition in a mutual embrace of the Persons in the unity of the Essence. In this embrace, in the essential Unity of God, all inward spirits are one with God in the immersion of love; and are that same one which the Es-sence is in Itself, according to the mode of Eternal Bliss. And in this most high unity of the Divine Nature, the heavenly Father is origin and beginning of every work which is worked in heaven and on earth. And HE says in the deep-sunken hiddenness of the spirit: BEHOLD, THE BRIDEGROOM COMETH: GO YE OUT TO MEET HIM.

These words we will now explain and set forth in their relation to that superessential contemplation which is the source of all holiness, and of all perfection of life to which one may attain. Few men can attain to this Divine seeing, because of their own incapacity and the mysteriousness of the light in which one sees. And therefore no one will thoroughly understand the meaning of it by any learning or subtle consideration of his own; for all words, and all that may be learnt and understood in a creaturely way, are foreign to, and far below, the truth which I mean. But he who is united with God, and is enlightened in this truth, he is able to understand truth by itself. . . . And therefore, whosoever wishes to understand this must have died to himself, and must live in God, and must turn his gaze to the eternal light in the ground of his spirit, where the Hidden Truth reveals Itself without means. For our Heavenly Father wills that we should see; for He is the Father of Light, and this is why He utters eternally, with-out intermediary and without interruption, in the hidden-ness of our spirit, one unique and abysmal word, and no other. . . . And this word is none other than: BEHOLD.

And this is the coming forth and the birth of the Son of Eternal Light, in Whom all blessedness is known and seen.

1

Now if the spirit would see God with God in this Divine light without means, there needs must be on the part of man three things.

The first is that he must be perfectly ordered from without in all the virtues, and within must be unencumbered, and as empty of every outward work as if he did not work at all: for if his emptiness is troubled within by some work of virtue, he has an image; and as long as this endures within him, he cannot contemplate.

Secondly, he must inwardly cleave to God, with adhering intention and love, even as a burning and glowing fire which can never be quenched. As long as he feels himself to be in this state, he is able to contemplate.

Thirdly, he must have lost himself in a Waylessness and in a Darkness, in which all contemplative men wander in fruition and wherein they never again can find themselves in a creaturely way. In the abyss of this darkness, in which the loving spirit has died to itself, there begin the manifestation of God and eternal life. For in this darkness there shines and is born an incomprehensible Light, which is the Son of God, in Whom we behold eternal life. And in this Light one becomes seeing; and this Divine Light is given to the simple sight of the spirit, where the spirit receives the brightness which is God Himself, above all gifts and every creaturely activity, in the idle emptiness in which the spirit has lost itself through fruitive love, and where it receives without means the brightness of God, and is changed without interruption into that brightness which it receives. Behold, this mysterious brightness, in which one sees everything that one can desire according to the emptiness of the spirit: this brightness is so great that the loving contemplative, in his ground wherein he rests, sees and feels nothing but an incomprehensible Light; and through that Simple Nudity which enfolds all things, he finds himself, and feels himself, to be that same Light by which he sees, and nothing else.

And this is the first condition by which one becomes seeing in the Divine Light. Blessed are the eyes which are thus seeing, for they possess eternal life.

2

When we have thus become seeing, we can behold in joy the eternal coming of our Bridegroom; and that is the second point of which we would speak. What is the coming of our Bridegroom which is eternal? It is the new birth and a new enlightenment without interruption; for the ground from which the Light shines forth, and which is the Light itself, is life-giving and fruitful, and therefore the manifestation of the Eternal Light is renewed without ceasing in the hiddenness of the spirit. Behold, every creaturely work, and every exercise of virtue, must here cease; for here God works alone in the high nobility of the spirit. And here there is nothing but an eternal seeing and staring at that Light, by that Light, and in that Light. And the coming of the Bridegroom is so swift that He is perpetually coming, and yet dwelling within with unfathomable riches; and ever coming anew, in His Person, without interruption, with such new brightness that it seems as though he had never come before. For His coming consists, beyond time, in an eternal Now, which is ever received with new longings and new joy. Behold, the delight and the joy which this Bridegroom brings with Him in His coming are boundless and without measure, for they are Himself. And this is why the eyes with which

the spirit sees and gazes at its Bridegroom, have opened
so wide that they can never close again. For the spirit continues for ever to see and to stare at the secret manifestation of God. And the grasp of the spirit is opened so wide
for the coming in of the Bridegroom, that the spirit itself
becomes that Breadth Which it grasps. And so God is
grasped and beheld through God; wherein rests all our
blessedness. This is the second point: in which we receive,
without interruption, the eternal coming of our Bridegroom in our spirit.

3

Now the spirit of God says in the secret outpouring of
our spirit: Go YE OUT, in an eternal contemplation and
fruition, according to the way of God. All the riches which
are in God by nature we possess by way of love in God,
and God in us, through the unmeasured love which is the
Holy Ghost; for in this love one tastes of all one can
desire. And therefore through this love we are dead to ourselves, and have gone forth in loving immersion into
Waylessness and Darkness. There the spirit is embraced
by the Holy Trinity, and dwells forever within the superessential Unity, in rest and fruition. And in that same
Unity, according to Its fruitfulness, the Father dwells in
the Son, and the Son in the Father, and all creatures dwell
in Both. And this is above the distinction of the Persons;
for here by means of the reason we understand Fatherhood
and Sonhood as the life-giving fruitfulness of the Divine
Nature.

Here there arise and begin an eternal going out and an
eternal work which is without beginning; for here there is
a beginning without beginning. For, after the Almighty
Father had perfectly comprehended Himself in the ground
of His fruitfulness, so the Son, the Eternal Word of the

Father, came forth as the second Person in the Godhead. And, through the Eternal Birth, all creatures have come forth in eternity, before they were created in time. So God has seen and known them in Himself, according to distinction, in living ideas, and in an otherness from Himself; but not as something other in all ways, for all that is in God is God. This eternal going out and this eternal life, which we have and are in God eternally, without ourselves, is the cause of our created being in time. And our created being abides in the Eternal Essence, and is one with it in its essential existence. And this eternal life and being, which we have and are in the eternal Wisdom of God, is like unto God. For it has an eternal immanence in the Divine Essence, without distinction; and through the birth of the Son it has an eternal outflowing in a distinction and otherness, according to the Eternal Idea. And through these two points it is so like unto God that He knows and reflects Himself in this likeness without cessation, according to the Essence and according to the Persons. For, though even here there are distinction and otherness according to intellectual perception, yet this likeness is one with that same Image of the Holy Trinity, which is the wisdom of God and in which God beholds Himself and all things in an eternal Now, without before and after. In a single seeing He beholds Himself and all things. And this is the Image and the Likeness of God, and our Image and our Likeness; for in it God reflects Himself and all things. In this Divine Image all creatures have an eternal life, outside themselves, as in their eternal Archetype; and after this eternal Image, and in this Likeness, we have been made by the Holy Trinity. And therefore God wills that we shall go forth from ourselves in this Divine Light, and shall reunite ourselves in a supernatural way with this Image, which is our proper life, and shall possess it with Him, in action and in fruition, in eternal bliss.

For we know well that the bosom of the Father is our ground and origin, in which we begin our being and our life. And from our proper ground, that is, from the Father and from all that lives in Him, there shines forth an eternal brightness, which is the birth of the Son. And in this brightness, that is, in the Son, the Father knows Himself and all that lives in Him; for all that He has, and all that He is, He gives to the Son, save only the property of Fatherhood, which abides in Himself. And this is why all that lives in the Father, unmanifested in the Unity, is also in the Son actively poured forth into manifestation: and the simple ground of our Eternal Image ever remains in darkness and in waylessness, but the brightness without limit which streams forth from it, this reveals and brings forth within the Conditioned the hiddenness of God. And all those men who are raised up above their created being into a God-seeing life are one with this Divine brightness. And they are that brightness itself, and they see, feel, and find, even by means of this Divine Light, that, as regards their uncreated essence, they are that same onefold ground from which the brightness without limit shines forth in the Divine way, and which, according to the simplicity of the Essence, abides eternally onefold and wayless within. And this is why inward and God-seeing men will go out in the way of contemplation, above reason and above distinction and above their created being, through an eternal intuitive gazing. By means of this inborn light they are transfigured, and made one with that same light through which they see and which they see. And thus the God-seeing men follow after their Eternal Image, after which they have been made; and they behold God in all things, without distinction, in a simple seeing, in the Divine

brightness. And this is the most noble and the most profitable contemplation to which one can attain in this life;
for in this contemplation, a man best remains master of
himself and free. And at each loving introversion he may
grow in nobility of life beyond anything that we are able
to understand; for he remains free and master of himself
in inwardness and virtue. And this gazing at the Divine
Light holds him up above all inwardness and all virtue
and all merit, for it is the crown and the reward after
which we strive, and which we have and possess now in
this wise; for a God-seeing life is a heavenly life. But were
we set free from this misery and this exile, so we should
have, as regards our created being, a greater capacity to
receive this brightness; and so the glory of God would
shine through us in every way better and more nobly. This
is the way above all ways, in which one goes out through
Divine contemplation and an eternal and intuitive gazing,
and in which one is transfigured and transmuted in the
Divine brightness. This going out of the God-seeing man
is also in love; for through the fruition of love he rises
above his created being, and finds and tastes the riches
and the delights which are God Himself, and which He
causes to pour forth without interruption in the hiddenness of the spirit, where the spirit is like unto the nobility
of God.

4

When the inward and God-seeing man has thus attained
to his Eternal Image, and in this clearness, through the
Son, has entered into the bosom of the Father: then he is
enlightened by Divine truth, and receives anew, every
moment, the Eternal Birth, and he goes forth according to
the way of the light, in a Divine contemplation. And here
there begins the fourth and last point; namely, a loving

meeting, in which, above all else, our highest blessedness consists.

You should know that the heavenly Father, as a living ground, with all that lives in Him, is actively turned towards His Son, as to His own Eternal Wisdom. And that same Wisdom, with all that lives in It, is actively turned back towards the Father, that is, towards that very ground from which It comes forth. And in this meeting there comes forth the third Person, between the Father and the Son; that is the Holy Ghost, Their mutual Love, who is one with them Both in the same nature. And He enfolds and drenches through both in action and fruition the Father and the Son, and all that lives in Both, with such great riches and such joy that as to this all creatures must eternally be silent; for the incomprehensible wonder of this love eternally transcends the understanding of all creatures. But where this wonder is understood and tasted without amazement, there the spirit dwells above itself, and is one with the Spirit of God; and tastes and sees without measure, even as God, the riches which are the spirit itself in the unity of the living ground, where it possesses itself according to the way of its uncreated essence.

Now this rapturous meeting is incessantly and actively renewed in us, according to the way of God; for the Father gives Himself in the Son, and the Son gives Himself in the Father, in an eternal content and a loving embrace; and this renews itself every moment within the bonds of love. For like as the Father incessantly beholds all things in the birth of His Son, so all things are loved anew by the Father and the Son in the outpouring of the Holy Ghost. And this is the active meeting of the Father and of the Son, in which we are lovingly embraced by the Holy Ghost in eternal love.

Now this active meeting and this loving embrace are in

their ground fruitive and wayless; for the abysmal Way-lessness of God is so dark and so unconditioned that it swallows up in itself every Divine way and activity, and all the attributes of the Persons, within the rich compass of the essential Unity; and it brings about a Divine frui-tion in the abyss of the Ineffable. And here there is a death in fruition, and a melting and dying into the Essential Nudity, where all the Divine names, and all conditions, and all the living images which are reflected in the mirror of Divine Truth, lapse in the Onefold and Ineffable, in waylessness and without reason. For in this unfathomable abyss of the Simplicity, all things are wrapped in fruitive bliss; and the abyss itself may not be comprehended, unless by the Essential Unity. To this the Persons, and all that lives in God, must give place; for here there is nought else but an eternal rest in the fruitive embrace of an out-pouring Love.

> And this is that wayless being which all interior spirits
>   have chosen above all other things.
> This is the dark silence in which all lovers lose them-
>   selves.
> But if we would prepare ourselves for it by means of
>   the virtues,
> We should strip ourselves of all but our very bodies,
> And should flee forth into the wild Sea,
> Whence no created thing can draw us back again.

May we possess in fruition the essential Unity, and clearly behold unity in the Trinity; this may Divine Love, which turns no beggar away, bestow upon us. AMEN.

Jan van Ruysbroeck

Prayer to God, the Holy Spirit

Come, true light,
Come, eternal life,
Come, secret of hiddenness.
Come, delight that has no name.
Come, unutterableness.
Come, O presence, forever fleeing from human nature.
Come, everlasting jubilee.
Come, light without end.
Come, awaited by all who are in want.
Come, resurrection of the dead.
Come, mighty one, forever creating, recreating, and renewing
    with a mere wave of Thy hand.
Come, Thou who remainest wholly invisible, for none ever to
    grasp or to caress.
Come, Thou who flowest in the river of hours,
       yet immovably stayest above it,
       who dwellest above all heavens,
       yet bendest to us who are bowed down.
Come, most longed-for and most hallowed name:
       to express what Thou art,
       to comprehend how Thou art, and how thou existest
       is forever denied to us.
Come, perpetual joy.
Come, unwitherable wreath.
Come, O purple raiment of our Lord and God.
Come, girdle, clear as crystal and many-coloured with precious
    gems.
Come, inaccessible refuge.

Come, Thou whom my poor soul desireth and hath desired.

Come, lonely one, to the lonely one—for lonely I am, as Thou canst see.

Come, Thou who hast made me solitary and forlorn on earth.

Come, Thou who hast become my longing, for that thou hast ordained,

> that I must needs long for Thee whom no human breath has ever reached.

Come, my breath and my life.

Come, joy, glory, and my incessant delight.

I give Thee thanks that without merging or losing Thyself in my nature, Thou art yet one spirit with me, and while Thou remainest God, high above everything, Thou hast become everything to me.

Ineffable nourishment, never to be withdrawn, pouring forth unceasingly into the lips of my spirit and aboundingly filling my inner self!

I give Thee thanks that Thou hast become for me a day without evening and a sun without setting:

Thou, who hast no place to hide, as Thou fillest the universe with Thy power.

Never hast Thou hidden from anyone; we, however, hide from Thee always, if we dare not appear before Thy face.

And where also shouldst Thou hide, Who hast nowhere a place to rest?

Or why shouldst Thou hide, Who dost not shrink nor shy away from anything in all the world?

Ah, Holy Lord—make an abode in me, dwell in me, and till my departure leave me not, leave not your servant;

That I too, may find myself after death in Thee, and reign with Thee, O God, who reignest over everything.

Remain with me, Lord, do not forsake me.

Strengthen me interiorly, so that I may be unmoved at all times, and protect me by dwelling in me: that, although dead, I may live in contemplating Thee, and although poor, may be rich in the possession of Thee.

Thus I shall be mightier than all kings:

Eating and drinking Thee, and at chosen hours wrapping myself in Thee, I shall enjoy unspeakable bliss.

For Thou art all Good, all Beauty, all Beatitude,
And Thine is the glory of the universe, Thine, with the Father and the Son, for ever and ever. Amen.

Symeon the New Theologian

The Ultimate Vision

O Virgin Mother, daughter of thy Son,
Humbler and more exalted than all others,
Predestined object of the eternal will!
Thou gavest such nobility to man
That He who made mankind did not disdain
To make Himself a creature of His making.
Within thy womb, that love was re-enkindled
Whose heat has germinated this fair flower,
To blossom thus in everlasting peace.
Thou art our noonday torch of charity;
And down below thou art for mortal men
The living fount of hope. Thou art so great,
O Lady, and thou art of so much worth,

That whoso hopes for grace, not knowing thee,
Asks that his wish should fly without its wings.
And thy benignity not only gives
Its succor to the suppliant, but oftentimes
Will lavishly anticipate his plea.
In thee is mercy, and magnificence,
And pity, for in thee is concentrate
Whatever good there be in any creature.
  "This man, who from the nethermost abyss
Of all the universe, as far as here,
Has seen the spiritual existences,
Now asks thy grace, so thou wilt grant him strength
That he may with his eyes uplift himself
Still higher toward the ultimate salvation.
And I, who ne'er for my own vision burned
As I now burn for his, proffer to thee
All my prayers—and pray they may suffice—
That thou wilt scatter from him every cloud
Of his mortality, with thine own prayers,
So that the bliss supreme may be revealed.
And furthermore I beg of thee, O Queen
That hast the power to do whate'er thou wilt,
After his vision to keep his love still pure.
May thy protection quell his human passions!
Lo, Beatrice and many a blessed soul
Entreat thee, with clasped hands, to grant my wish!"
  Those eyes so loved and reverenced by God,
Were fixed upon the suppliant, and showed
How greatly She is pleased by earnest prayers.
Then they were turned to that eternal light
Whose depth, one must believe, no other eye
Has vision clear enough to penetrate.
  And I—who now was drawing near the end
Of all desires—ended, as was meet,

Within myself the ardor of my longing.
Here Bernard smiled and made a sign to me
That I should look on high; but I indeed
Was doing what he wished, of my own will,
Because my vision, being purified,
Was piercing more and more within the rays
Of light sublime, which in itself is true.
Thenceforward, no mere human speech could tell
My vision's added power: for memory
And speech are both o'ercome by such excess.

    Just as a man who sees things in a dream,
Will still retain impression of his feelings
Although the rest return not to his mind,
So now am I: for though my vision fades,
The sweetness growing from it yet distills
Its essence in the wellsprings of my heart.
Thus the snow is melted in the sun;
And thus the Sibyl's oracle was lost,
Written on leaves so light upon the wind.

    O Light Supreme, that art so far exalted
Above our mortal ken! Lend to my mind
A little part of what Thou didst appear,
And grant sufficient power unto my tongue
That it may leave for races yet unborn,
A single spark of Thy almighty flame!
For if Thou wilt come back to my remembrance,
That I may sing Thy glory in these lines,
The more Thy victory will be explained.

    I think the keenness of the living ray
That I withstood would have bewildered me,
If once my eyes had turned aside from it.
And I recall that for that very reason
I was emboldened to endure so much,
Until my gaze was joined unto His good.

Abundant grace, by which I could presume
To fix my eyes upon the Eternal Light
Sufficiently to see the whole of it!

I saw that in its depths there are enclosed,
Bound up with love in one eternal book,
The scattered leaves of all the universe—
Substance, and accidents, and their relations,
As though together fused in such a way
That what I speak of is a single light.
The universal form of this commingling
I think I saw, for when I tell of it
I feel that I rejoice so much the more.
One moment brought me more oblivion
Than five-and-twenty centuries could cast
Upon those Argonauts whose shadow once
Made Neptune wonder. Even thus my mind,
Enraptured, gazed attentive, motionless,
And grew the more enkindled as it gazed.

For in the presence of those radiant beams
One is so changed, that 'tis impossible
To turn from it to any other sight—
Because the good, the object of the will,
Is all collected there. Outside of it
That is defective which is perfect there.
Henceforth my speech will fall still further short
Of what I recollect, as 'twere a babe's,
Wetting his tongue upon his mother's breast.

There was no other than a single semblance
Within that Living Light on which I gazed,
For that remains forever what it was;
And yet by reason of my vision's power,
Which waxed the stronger in me as I looked,
That semblance seemed to change, and I as well.

For within the substance, deep and radiant,
Of that Exalted Light, I saw three rings
Of one dimension, yet of triple hue.
One seemed to be reflected by the next,
As Iris is by Iris; and the third
Seemed fire, shed forth equally by both.
How powerless is speech—how weak, compared
To my conception, which itself is trifling
Beside the mighty vision that I saw!

    O Light Eternal, in Thyself contained!
Thou only know'st Thyself, and in Thyself
Both known and knowing, smilest on Thyself!

    That very circle which appeared in Thee,
Conceived as but reflection of a light,
When I had gazed on it awhile, now seemed
To bear the image of a human face
Within itself, of its own coloring—
Wherefore my sight was wholly fixed on it.
Like a geometer, who will attempt
With all his power and mind to square the circle,
Yet cannot find the principle he needs:
Just so was I, at that phenomenon.
I wished to see how image joined to ring,
And how the one found place within the other.
Too feeble for such flights were my own wings;
But by a lightning flash my mind was struck—
And thus came the fulfilment of my wish.

    My power now failed that phantasy sublime:
My will and my desire were both revolved,
As is a wheel in even motion driven,
By Love, which moves the sun and other stars.

Dante

X
The Day Without Evening

And the Seventh keeps He within Him, for to give us in everlasting glory. If we wit it not now, we shall wit it when the body our soul leaves.

The Mirror of Simple Souls

The Holy Week of our Life

There is a day of yearning and of blissful joy,
                    in the Annunciation of Christ.
There is a day of rest and sweet tenderness,
                    in the Birth of Christ.
There is a day of troth and joyful union,
                    Holy Thursday.
There is a day of gentleness and innermost love,
                    Good Friday.
There is a day of power and high rejoicing,
                    Easter.
There is a day of faith and pitiful grief,
                    the Ascension.
There is a day of truth and burning consolation,
                    Pentecost.
There is a day of justice and of the true hour,
                    the Last Judgment.
There is a week of which we should spend seven days.
One, our Lord will spend with us all—the Last Day.

Mechthild of Magdeburg

The Goods He Hath Ordained to Give Us

I saw three manners of longing in God, and all to one end;
of which we have the same in us, and by the same virtue
and for the same end.

The first is, that He longeth to teach us to know Him and love Him evermore, as it is convenient and speedful to us. The second is, that He longeth to have us up to His Bliss, as souls are when they are taken out of pain into Heaven. The third is to fulfill us in bliss; and that shall be on the Last Day, fulfilled ever to last. For I saw, as it is known in our Faith, that the pain and the sorrow shall be ended to all that shall be saved. And not only shall we receive the same bliss that souls afore have had in Heaven, but also we shall receive a new [bliss], which plenteously shall be flowing out of God into us and shall fulfill us; and these be the goods which He hath ordained to give us from without beginning. These goods are treasured and hid in Himself; for unto that time [no] Creature is mighty nor worthy to receive them.

In this [fulfilling] we shall see verily the cause of all things that He hath done; and evermore we shall see the cause of all things that He hath suffered. And the bliss and the fulfilling shall be so deep and so high that, for wonder and marvel, all creatures shall have to God so great reverent dread, overpassing that which hath been seen and felt before, that the pillars of heaven shall tremble and quake. But this manner of trembling and dread shall have no pain; but it belongeth to the worthy might of God thus to be beholden by His creatures, in great trembling and quaking for meekness of joy, marvelling at the greatness of God the Maker and at the littleness of all that is made. For the beholding of this maketh the creature marvellously meek and mild.

Wherefore God willeth—and also it belongeth to us, both in nature and grace—that we wit and know of this, desiring this sight and this working; for it leadeth us in right way, and keepeth us in true life, and oneth us to God. And as good as God is, so great He is; and as much as it belongeth to His goodness to be loved, so much it belongeth to His greatness to be dreaded. For this reverent dread is the fair courtesy that is in Heaven afore God's face. And as much as He shall then be known and loved overpassing that He is now, in so much He shall be dreaded overpassing that He is now. Wherefore it behoveth needs to be that all Heaven and earth shall tremble and quake when the pillars shall tremble and quake.

Juliana of Norwich

The Last Things

And your voice speaks:
But when once the Great End of all mysteries shall begin,
When the Hidden One shall blaze forth in terrible storms of
      unfettered love,
When His home-call shall rend the welkin like a tempest and
      the wasted desire of His creation shall shout for joy,
When the bodies of the stars burst into flame and out of their
      ashes light shall rise delivered,
When the heavy dykes of matter break and open all the sluices
      of the invisible,
When decades of centuries sweep back like eagles, and em-
      battled aeons come home to eternity,
When the vessels of speech shall be shattered, and torrents of
      the never uttered shall burst forth,
When the loneliest souls are washed up into the light, and see
      there what they never knew about themselves;
Then will the Revealed One raise my head, and before His
      sight all my veils will rise in flames,

And I shall lie there like a naked mirror in the presence of all
worlds.

And the stars will find in me their praises, and the ages will
find in me their eternity, and the souls will find in me
their divinity.

And God will recognize in me His love.

And henceforth my head shall wear no other veil than the
dazzling light of Him who is my judge.

The world will be lost in this veil of light.

And the veil shall be called mercy, and mercy shall be called
infinite.

And the Infinite shall be called blessedness. Amen.

Gertrud von Le Fort

The Day Without Evening

O Lord God, grant us peace, for Thou hast granted us all
things, the peace of repose, the peace of Thy Sabbath, the
peace that has no evening. For this gloriously beautiful
order of things that are very good will pass away when it
has achieved its end: it will have its morning and its
evening.

But the seventh day is without evening. It has no sunset,
for You sanctified it that it may abide forever. After all
Your works which were very good, You rested on the seventh day—although You made them with no interruption
of Your repose. And likewise the voice of Your Book tells
us that we also, after our works—which are only very good
because You have granted us to accomplish them—will rest
in You in the Sabbath of life everlasting.

For then also You will rest in us, as now You operate in us, so that it will be Your rest in us as it is now Your work in us. But You, Lord, are ever in action and ever at rest. You do not see in time nor move in time nor rest in time. Yet You make the things we see in time, and You make both time while time is and rest when time is no more.

We see the things You have made, because they are; and they are, because You see them. Looking outside ourselves we see that they are, and looking into our own mind we see that they are good: but You saw them as made when You saw that they were to be made.

At the present time we move towards doing good, since our heart has so conceived by Your Spirit; but at an earlier time we moved towards doing ill, for we had gone away from You. But You, God, who alone are good, have never ceased to do good. Some indeed of our works are good through Your grace, but they are not eternal: after them we hope that we shall find rest in the greatness of Your sanctification. But You, the Good, who need no good beside, are ever in repose, because You are Your own repose.

What man will give another man the understanding of this, or what angel will give another angel, or what angel will give a man? Of You we must ask, in You we must seek, at You we must knock. Thus only shall we receive, thus shall we find, thus will it be opened to us.

St. Augustine

Finale Maestoso

Eucharistia

Right indeed is it and just, that we should give thanks to Thee,
Glorify Thee and praise Thee, God, Father of heaven and
  earth,
Together with Thy Incarnate Son and the Holy Spirit.
Thine, O God, are all creatures in heaven and earth and they
  incessantly glorify Thee.
The sun heralds Thee, the moon reveres Thee and all celestial
  bodies highly praise Thee.
The seas extoll Thee and everything that is in them.
The earth, truly Thy footstool, worships Thee.
She glorifies Thy Godhead in the Holy Church, who offers pure
  hymns through the mouth of Thy children:
Through the foretelling of prophets,
Through the hosts of apostles,
Through the death and stoning of martyrs,
Through the last breath of confessors,
Through the wisdom of doctors,
Through the glorious virtues of hermits,
Through the burden and toil of those who suffer poverty vol-
  untarily,
Through the number of the just,
Through the joyous songs of virgins,
Through the sighs of those who suffer persecution,
Through the tears of penitents,
Further through every generation of the faithful.
The heavens also praise Thee, arranged in three hierarchies;
There Thou art extolled, exalted, and praised:

Through psalms ever renewed,
Through pure and holy hymns,
Through the sweet sounds of the harp and delightful songs of
     praise,
Through triumphant and solemn chants, never silent and never
     ending,
Through the glowing flames of fiery voices,
Where thousand times thousand and myriad times myriad sing
     perpetual hymns of praise,
Not with human but with flaming tongues . . .
Through the sweetest melodies of angels,
Through the jubilant harmonies of archangels,
Through the sonorous voices of Principalities,
Through the splendour of Powers,
Through the awe-inspiring calls of Dominations,
Through the warriors of the heavenly Virtues,
Through the most elect canticles of the Thrones,
Through the fearful thunder of the Cherubim,
Through the burning wings of the six-winged Seraphim,
Who sing, cry, shout and speak forever with one and the same
     voice of jubilation:

HOLY, HOLY, HOLY!

Anaphora of the Syrian Liturgy

Sources

Aegidius of Assisi
In Menge, Gisbert, O.F.M., *Der selige Aegidius von Assisi: Sein Leben und seine Sprüche,* Paderborn, 1906.

Anselm of Canterbury, St.
Proslogium. Translated by Sidney Norton Deane. Chicago: Open Court Publishing Co., 1903.

Augustine, St.
The Confessions of St. Augustine. Translated by F. J. Sheed. New York: Sheed & Ward, 1950.

Bernard of Clairvaux, St.
St. Bernard on the Love of God. Translated by T. L. Connolly, S.J. Westminster, Md.: Newman Press, 1951.

Camus, Jean Pierre
The Spirit of St. François de Sales. Edited and translated with an introduction by C. F. Kelley. New York: Harper & Bros., 1952.

Cloud of Unknowing and Other Treatises, The
By an English mystic of the fourteenth century. With a commentary on *The Cloud* . . . by Augustin Baker, O.S.B. Edited by Justin McCann. London: Burns, Oates & Washbourne, Ltd., 1936.

Dante Alighieri
The Divine Comedy. Translated by Lawrence Grant White. New York: Pantheon Books, 1948.

D'Arcy, M. C., S.J.
The Mind and Heart of Love. New York: Henry Holt & Co., 1947.
In *The Poems of St. John of the Cross,* translated by Roy Campbell, Preface.

Dionysius the Areopagite
De divinis nominibus; De mystica theologia. Version of Joannes Scotus (Erigena). In Migne, J. P., *Patrologia Latina,* vol. CXXII, 1853.

Eckhart, Meister Johann
In Blakney, R. B., *Meister Eckhart: A Modern Translation,* New York and London: Harper & Bros., 1941.

Gratry, A[uguste Joseph Alphonse]
Philosophie: De la connaissance de l'âme. Paris: C. Douniol, 1857.

Lavelle, Louis
The Meaning of Holiness as exemplified in St. Francis of Assisi, St. Teresa of Avila, St. John of the Cross, and St. Francis de Sales. Translated by Dorothea O'Sullivan. New York: Pan-

theon Books, Inc., 1954.

Hopkins, Gerard Manley
Poems. New York and London: Oxford University Press, 1948.

Jacopone da Todi
In Underhill, Evelyn, *Jacopone da Todi, Poet and Mystic—1228-1306: A Spiritual Biography,* with a selection from the spiritual songs ... translated by Mrs. Theodore Beck, New York: E. P. Dutton & Co., 1919.

John Climacus, St.
In Arseniew, Nicolas von, *Ostkirche und Mystik,* Munich: Ernst Reinhardt, 1925.

John of the Cross, St.
The Ascent of Mount Carmel. Translated by David Lewis. With corrections and a prefatory essay on the development of mysticism in the Carmelite order, by Benedict Zimmerman. London: T. Baker, 1932.
The Poems of St. John of the Cross. Translated by Roy Campbell. With a preface by M. C. D'Arcy, S.J. New York: Pantheon Books, Inc., 1951.
In Huxley, Aldous, *The Perennial Philosophy,* New York and London: Harper & Bros., 1945.

Joinville, Jean de
The Life of St. Louis. Translated by René Hague, from the text edited by Natalis de Wailly. Makers of Christendom Series, edited by Christopher Dawson. New York: Sheed & Ward, 1955.

Juliana of Norwich
Revelations of Divine Love. From the manuscript in the British Museum, edited by G. Warrack. Westminster, Md.: Newman Press, 1952.

Le Fort, Gertrud von
Hymns to the Church. Translated by Margaret Chanler. New York: Sheed & Ward, 1953.

León, Luis de
In Peers, E. Allison, *The Mystics of Spain,* Ethical and Religious Classics of the East and West, No. 5, London: G. Allen & Unwin, 1951.

Loyola, Ignatius, St.
In Broderick, James, S.J., *St. Ignatius Loyola,* New York: Farrar, Straus & Cudahy, Inc., 1956.

Lull, Ramón
The Book of the Lover and the Beloved. In Peers, E. Allison, *The Mystics of Spain,* Ethical and Religious Classics of the East and West,

No. 5, London: G. Allen & Unwin, 1951.

Mechthild of Magdeburg
Offenbarungen der Schwester Mechthild von Magdeburg, oder Das fliessende Licht der Gottheit. From the Einsiedeln Ms., edited by Gall Morel, O.S.B., Regensburg: G. T. Manz, 1869.

Merton, Thomas
Seeds of Contemplation. New York: New Directions, 1949.

Nicholas of Cusa
The Vision of God. Translated by Emma Gurney Salter, with an introduction by Evelyn Underhill. New York: E. P. Dutton & Co., 1928.

Roman Liturgy
Holy Saturday Mass: Blessing of the Fire. From *The Missal in Latin and English,* New York: Sheed & Ward, 1953.

Ruysbroeck, Jan van
The Adornment of the Spiritual Marriage [etc.]. Translated from the Flemish by C. A. Wynschenk. Edited with an introduction and notes by Evelyn Underhill. New York: E. P. Dutton & Co., 1916.

Suso, Heinrich
The Life of Blessed Henry Suso by Himself. Translated by T. F. Knox. London: Methuen & Co., Ltd., 1913.

Symeon (the New Theologian)
Simeonis Junioris . . . Orationes XXXIII—Divinorum amorum sive sacrarum commentationum liber singularis. In Migne, J. P., *Patrologia Graeca-Latina,* vol. CXX, 1857.

Syrian Liturgy
Anaphora: Eucharistia. From *Ecclesia Orans,* Zur Einführung in den Geist der Liturgie. Edited by Dr. Ildefons Herwegen. Vol. X, "Die Liturgie als Quelle östlicher Frömmigkeit," by Julius Tyciac. Freiburg i.Br.: Herder & Co., 1937.

Tauler, Johannes
Die Predigten Taulers. From the Engelberg and Freiburg Mss., with Schmidt's transcriptions of the formerly existent Strasbourg Mss., edited by F. Vetter. Berlin: Weidman, 1910.

Thomas of Celano
The Lives of S. Francis of Assisi. Translated by A. G. Ferrers Howell. New York: E. P. Dutton & Co., 1908.

Vincent de Paul, St.
In Maynard, M. U., *Virtues and Spiritual Doctrine of St. Vincent de Paul,* trans-

lated from the French by a priest of the Congregation of the Mission, Suspension Bridge, Buffalo, N.Y.: Niagara Index Publishing House, 1877.

William of Saint-Thierry
The Golden Epistle of Abbot William of Saint-Thierry to the Carthusians of Mont Dieu. Translated by Walter Shewring; edited by Justin McCann. London: Sheed & Ward, 1930.